NETWORK
CHECKLIST

When you plan to connect your laptop to a network at your destination, here are some questions to ask before you leave on your trip:

- What network operating system and topology (network design) will you be working on?
- Which network shell and device drivers do you need to attach to the local area network?
- Should the CONFIG.SYS and AUTOEXEC.BAT files be modified to get onto the network smoothly?
- How do you get into the system after the hardware has made the connection?
- Will the default log-in directory, password identification, file, directory, and user group access rights be established before you arrive? If not, who do you contact to set this up? If so, what are they?
- Will your access rights allow you to use network resources such as printers and shared directories?
- Will there be a menu system to work from? If not, what are the specific locations of programs and files you will need to access? If so, how does the menu system work?
- What is the proper way to log off the network?

Computer users are not all alike.
Neither are SYBEX books.

We know our customers have a variety of needs. They've told us so. And because we've listened, we've developed several distinct types of books to meet the needs of each of our customers. What are you looking for in computer help?

If you're looking for the basics, try the **ABC's** series, or for a more visual approach, select **Teach Yourself**.

Mastering and **Understanding** titles offer you a step-by-step introduction, plus an in-depth examination of intermediate-level features, to use as you progress.

Our **Up & Running** series is designed for computer-literate consumers who want a no-nonsense overview of new programs. Just 20 basic lessons, and you're on your way.

SYBEX **Encyclopedias** and **Desktop References** provide a *comprehensive reference* and explanation of all of the commands, features and functions of the subject software.

Sometimes a subject requires a special treatment that our standard series doesn't provide. So you'll find we have titles like **Advanced Techniques, Handbooks, Tips & Tricks**, and others that are specifically tailored to satisfy a unique need.

You'll find SYBEX publishes a variety of books on every popular software package. Looking for computer help? Help Yourself to SYBEX.

For a complete catalog of our publications:

SYBEX Inc.
2021 Challenger Drive, Alameda, CA 94501
Tel: (510) 523-8233/(800) 227-2346 Telex: 336311
Fax: (510) 523-2373

SYBEX is committed to using natural resources wisely to preserve and improve our environment. This is why we have been printing the text of books like this one on recycled paper since 1982.

This year our use of recycled paper will result in the saving of more than 15,300 trees. We will lower air pollution effluents by 54,000 pounds, save 6,300,000 gallons of water, and reduce landfill by 2,700 cubic yards.

In choosing a SYBEX book you are not only making a choice for the best in skills and information, you are also choosing to enhance the quality of life for all of us.

The Laptop User's Survival Guide

The Laptop User's Survival Guide

Jeffrey H. Lubeck
Bruce D. Schatzman

SYBEX®

San Francisco ■ Paris ■ Düsseldorf ■ Soest

Acquisitions Editor: David Clark
Editor: Marilyn Smith
Project Editor: Kathleen Lattinville
Technical Editor: Jason Roberts
Word Processors: Ann Dunn, Susan Trybull
Book Designer: Ingrid Owen
Chapter Art: Ingrid Owen
Production Artist/Coordinator: Suzanne Albertson
Technical Art: Rick van Genderen
Screen Graphics: Cuong Le
Typesetter: Dharma Enterprises
Proofreader/Production Coordinator: Rhonda Holmes
Indexer: Ted Laux
Cover Designer: Ingalls + Associates
Cover Photographer: Mark Johann

SYBEX is a registered trademark of SYBEX, Inc.

TRADEMARKS: SYBEX has attempted throughout this book to distinguish proprietary trademarks from descriptive terms by following the capitalization style used by the manufacturer.

SYBEX is not affiliated with any manufacturer.

Every effort has been made to supply complete and accurate information. However, SYBEX assumes no responsibility for its use, nor for any infringement of the intellectual property rights of third parties which would result from such use.

Copyright © 1991 SYBEX Inc., 2021 Challenger Drive, Alameda, CA 94501. World rights reserved. No part of this publication may be stored in a retrieval system, transmitted, or reproduced in any way, including but not limited to photocopy, photograph, magnetic or other record, without the prior agreement and written permission of the publisher.

Library of Congress Card Number: 91-65588
ISBN: 0-89588-863-7

Manufactured in the United States of America
10 9 8 7 6 5 4 3 2 1

This book is dedicated to our wives,
Linda and Debra.

ACKNOWLEDGMENTS

We would like to acknowledge the following people for their contributions:

David Clark

George Dart

Dennis Frahmann

Kathleen Lattinville

Jason Roberts

Marilyn Smith

Rick van Genderen

CONTENTS AT A GLANCE

INTRODUCTION   xxv

CHAPTER

1	Essential Battle Gear for Success	1
2	Making the Most of Your Laptop Hardware	17
3	Managing Disk Space	29
4	Exchanging Files on the Road	39
5	Using Utility Packages to Avoid Disaster	49
6	Printing on the Road	59
7	Laptop-to-Desktop File Transfer	71
8	Effective Remote Communications	77
9	Connecting Your Laptop to a Local Area Network	95
10	Faxing on the Road	105
11	Working in Hostile Environments	123
12	Extra Tips for You and Your Laptop	133
13	Quick Guide to Application Commands	147

APPENDICES

A	Guide to Product Sources	199
B	Glossary of Common Terms	209
C	Creating Traveling Versions of Your Applications	217
	INDEX	223

CONTENTS

INTRODUCTION xxv

ONE

Essential Battle Gear for Success   1

Longer Power Cords for Work Area Flexibility	2
Improve Your Modem Capabilities with Longer Telephone Cables	3
Bring Extra Battery Packs for an Additional Power Source	4
Maximize the Power of Your Pointing Device	5
Fluent Communication with Multipurpose Modems	7
Quick Changes in Power Connections	9
All Dressed Up and Nowhere to Print	10
Eliminate the Floppy Disk Size Controversy	11
Take Advantage of a Network Connection	12
Keep Critical Programs and Files on Floppy Disks to Avoid Disaster	14
Making a Case for Cases	15
Sort Out What You Really Need	15
Battle Gear Check List	16

Survival Tips

BATTLE GEAR TIP #1: Bring a 12-Foot Power Cord	3
BATTLE GEAR TIP #2: Bring a Long Phone Cable	4
BATTLE GEAR TIP #3: Double Your Power	5
BATTLE GEAR TIP #4: Buy Another Pointing Device	5
BATTLE GEAR TIP #5: Get a Fax Modem	7
BATTLE GEAR TIP #6: Bring a 3-to-2 Adapter	9
BATTLE GEAR TIP #7: Take Printer Cables	10
BATTLE GEAR TIP #8: Bring a Transfer Program and Cable	12
BATTLE GEAR TIP #9: Buy a Networking Device	13
BATTLE GEAR TIP #10: Take Backup Copies	14
BATTLE GEAR TIP #11: Put It All in a Case	15

TWO

Making the Most of Your Laptop Hardware — 17

Your Laptop's Environment	18
Increase Your RAM Capacity	20
Prepare for Different Monitor Requirements	23
Use Expansion Slots Wisely	26

Survival Tips

RAM TIP #1: Use a Memory Manager for Additional Memory	21
RAM TIP #2: Remove Unnecessary Device Drivers	22
MONITOR TIP #1: Be Ready for VGA	25
EXPANSION SLOT TIP #1: Use Slots for Fax, Modem, or Network Board	26

THREE

Managing Disk Space — 29

Maximizing Your Hard Disk Space	30
Using Utilities to Defragment and Compress Files	33
Managing Your Windows Swap File	35

Survival Tips

HARD DISK TIP #1: Compress Files with the Save As Command	30
HARD DISK TIP #2: Remove Unnecessary Files	31
DISK UTILITY TIP #1: Use a Defragmentation Utility	33
DISK UTILITY TIP #2: Compress and Archive Selected Files	34
SWAP FILE TIP #1: Adjust the Size of Your Windows 3.0 Swap File	35

FOUR

Exchanging Files on the Road — 39

Sharing Files with Other Applications	40
Importing File Information	41
Exporting Data to Another Application	43
Transferring Font Information	46

Survival Tips

FILE SHARING TIP #1: Use Applications that Support Standard Formats — 43

FILE SHARING TIP #2: Get a Few Widely Used Applications — 46

FIVE

Using Utility Packages to Avoid Disaster — 49

DOS Can Provide Some Utility Answers	50
The Jack of All Trades	52
Hard-Disk-Management Utilities Revisited	54
Getting Files to and from Your Laptop Faster	55

Keeping Your Files Clean	56
Reading the File Once You Get It	57

Survival Tips

DOS UTILITY TIP #1: Upgrade to MS-DOS 5.0	51
TOOLKIT TIP #1: Have a Format Disaster Plan	53
TOOLKIT TIP #2: Avoid the DEL *.* Blues	53
TOOLKIT TIP #3: Find the Needle in the Haystack	53
FILE MOVEMENT TIP #1: Use a Transfer Utility	55
CLEANSING UTILITY TIP #1: Protect Your Files from Viruses	56
READING TIP #1: Get a File-Conversion Utility	57

SIX

Printing on the Road — 59

Avoiding Show Stoppers	60
What You Get Is Not What You Want	65

Survival Tips

PRINTING TIP #1: Battle Gear Tip #7 Revisited	61
PRINTING TIP #2: Take an Interface Converter	62
PRINTING TIP #3: Take a Variety of Printer Drivers	62

PRINTING TIP #4: Confirm that You'll Have Enough Printer Memory	64
WYSIWYG TIP #1: Make Sure Your Application Can Control Page Setup	66
WYSIWYG TIP #2: Use Soft Fonts for Font Support	66
WYSIWYG TIP #3: Forget about Printer Cartridges	68

SEVEN

Laptop-to-Desktop File Transfer 71

Transferring Large Amounts of Data 72
Using LapLink on the Road 74

Survival Tips

HEFTY TRANSFER TIP #1: Use a Utility Instead of a Disk Drive	73
HEFTY TRANSFER TIP #2: Maintain Mirrored Directories	73

EIGHT

Effective Remote Communications — 77

Configuring Your Laptop for Remote Communication	78
Your Slot Options	79
The Importance of How Your Modem Operates	80
Getting Maximum Performance from Your Modem	83
Finding the Proper Software Solution	89
Making Sure the Host and Remote Machines Can Communicate	91

Survival Tips

REMOTE CONNECTIVITY TIP #1: Uniformity Can Be an Advantage	78
REMOTE CONNECTIVITY TIP #2: Avoid Using an Expansion Chassis	79
MODEM TIP #1: Use an Internal Modem	81
MODEM TIP #2: Make Your Modem Work Properly with Windows	81
MODEM TIP #3: Purchase a Powerful Modem	84
MODEM TIP #4: Get a Modem with Built-in Error Control	85
MODEM TIP #5: Shorten Your Transfer Time by Using Data Compression	86
MODEM SOFTWARE TIP #1: Select Software that Provides Error Control and Data Compression	89

MODEM SOFTWARE TIP #2: Turn Off Your Software Features If Your Modem Already Has Them	90
MODEM SOFTWARE TIP #3: Use Software that Provides Remote Control of Another Machine	90

NINE

Connecting Your Laptop to a Local Area Network — 95

The Zero-Slot Approach	96
The External LAN Adapter Approach	99
Expansion Chassis: The Expensive Alternative	100
The Network Interface Card Approach	101
Getting to Work after Making the Connection	102

Survival Tips

ZERO-SLOT TIP #1: Packages Are Inexpensive and Simple to Use	97
ZERO-SLOT TIP #2: Answer Some Questions before Buying a Package	98
LAN ADAPTER TIP #1: External Adapters Provide Power in Your Hand	99
INTERFACE CARD TIP #1: Proprietary Network Cards Offer Power with No Flexibility	101
INTERFACE CARD TIP #2: Standard Network Cards Are the First Choice for Full Connection	102

TEN

Faxing on the Road — 105

The Fax Machine Alternatives	106
Fax Features for Travelers	111
Faxing on the Road with Desktop Units	112
Faxing on the Road with a Portable Fax Machine	114
Faxing on the Road with an Internal or Serial-Port Device	114
Faxing on the Road Using Your Modem and a Bulletin Board Fax Service	119
Receiving Faxes on the Road	120

Survival Tips

FAX TYPE TIP #1: Use Desktop Fax Machines to Send Hard Copies	107
FAX TYPE TIP #2: Portable, Stand-Alone Fax Machines Are Not That Portable	108
FAX TYPE TIP #3: Internal Fax-Modem Boards Are the Choice for the Frequent Traveler	108
FAX TYPE TIP #4: Pocket-Size, Serial-Port Devices Pack Functionality into a Small Space	109
FAX FEATURE TIP #1: Fax while You Sleep	111
FAX FEATURE TIP #2: Broadcast Your Messages	112
FAX FEATURE TIP #3: Fax with the Ease of Printing	112
DESKTOP FAXING TIP #1: Check the Availability of the Machine	113
DESKTOP FAXING TIP #2: Know Where You Will Print	113

INTERNAL OR SERIAL-PORT FAXING TIP #1: Hand-Held Scanners Provide Hard Copies on the Spot	115
INTERNAL OR SERIAL-PORT FAXING TIP #2: Use Printer Redirection to Send Formatted Documents	115
INTERNAL OR SERIAL-PORT FAXING TIP #3: ASCII Format Works with Most Faxes	118
INTERNAL OR SERIAL-PORT FAXING TIP #4: Some Devices Work with Graphics	119
FAX RECEIPT TIP #1: Convert the Fax to PCX to Bring It into a Document	120
FAX RECEIPT TIP #2: Compress Your Fax Files	122

ELEVEN

Working in Hostile Environments   123

A Call-Ahead Check List	124
Taking Control in Hotel/Motel Rooms	125
Hooking Up to a Telephone	127
Working in Airports	129

Survival Tips

HOTEL/MOTEL TIP #1: Bring Along the Proper Battle Gear	126
TELEPHONE HOOKUP TIP #1: Bring a Communications Kit	127

TELEPHONE HOOKUP TIP #2: Use a Device to Connect to Any Telephone	128
AIRPORT TIP #1: Find a Work Area	130
AIRPORT TIP #2: Get through Airport Security Safely	130

TWELVE

Extra Tips for You and Your Laptop — 133

Floppy Disk Drive Compatibility	134
Prolonging the Life of Your Laptop's Batteries	137
Backing Up Your Data on the Road	142
Information Resources for Traveling Laptop Users	144

Survival Tips

FLOPPY DRIVE TIP #1: The Disk with the Data You Want to Import May Not Be Compatible with Your Laptop	135
FLOPPY DRIVE TIP #2: The Disk with the Data You Want to Export May Not Be Compatible with the Other Computer	136
BATTERY SAVING TIP #1: Lower Your Screen's Light Output	138
BATTERY SAVING TIP #2: Use a Disk Cache to Make Your Floppy and Hard Disk Drives Work Less	139
BATTERY SAVING TIP #3: Set Up a RAM Disk for Large Applications	139

BATTERY SAVING TIP #4: Use AC Power for
Disk-Intensive Work   141

BACKUP STRATEGY TIP #1: Use Floppies, PKZIP, and
the DOS COPY Command for Simple Backups   142

BACKUP STRATEGY TIP #2: Bring Floppy Disks and
Professional Backup Software for More Complex
Backups   143

BACKUP STRATEGY TIP #3: Consider an External
Hard Drive for Big Backups   143

BACKUP STRATEGY TIP #4: Create a Backup before
You Leave   144

THIRTEEN

Quick Guide to Application Commands — 147

Commonly Used MS-DOS Commands   148
Windows Quick Keys   163
   Windows Program Manager Menu Key Sequences   163
   General Windows System Functions   165
   Manipulating Application Windows   165
   Working with Dialog Boxes   166
WordPerfect 5.1 Function Key Commands   167
   WordPerfect 5.1 Commands by Function   167
   WordPerfect 5.1 Commands by Key Sequence   169
MS Word 5.5 Function Key Commands   171
   MS Word 5.5 Commands by Function   171
   MS Word 5.5 Commands by Key Sequence   173

Twenty-Five Lotus 1-2-3 Commands	175
Excel for Windows Keystrokes and Commands	177
Excel Worksheet Cursor-Movement Keystrokes	177
Excel Worksheet Selection Keystrokes	178
Excel Formula Bar Keystrokes	179
Excel Function Key and Ctrl Key Shortcuts	180
Excel Cell Formatting Keystrokes	181
Excel Page Setup Dialog Box Header and Footer Codes	182
dBASE III Commands and Keystrokes	183
dBASE Keystroke Commands	188
PageMaker for Windows Commands	188
Crosstalk for Windows Commands	190
PC Tools 5.5 and 6.0 File and Disk Utilities	191
COMPRESS	192
DISKFIX	193
MIRROR	194
PCBACKUP	194
PCCACHE	196
REBUILD	198

APPENDIX A

Guide to Product Sources **199**

APPENDIX B

Glossary of Common Terms **209**

APPENDIX C

Creating Traveling Versions of Your Applications **217**

INDEX **223**

INTRODUCTION

This book is written for users of laptop computers, although much of the information here can benefit users of desktop personal computers. Laptops provide the greatest amount of computing power and flexibility in a truly portable package. This guide addresses the problems of using a laptop in various environments and offers suggestions for improving its performance.

The Portable Computing Revolution

The portable computing "revolution" was actually many years in the making. Between 1983 and 1984, computer manufacturers marketed the first of what were to become known as "portable" computers. Although a few had innovative designs, they were little more than desktop personal computers with handles. Most of these machines had small, hard-to-read screens; poor expandability; insufficient storage capacity; and unsatisfactory performance. These computers were quickly renamed "luggable" by users who never quite got used to their size and weight.

It was not until 1987 that portable computing became really portable. Sparked by advances in miniaturization and manufacturing technology, the first of the true laptops appeared, consisting of a totally redesigned CPU package, flat-screen (non-CRT) display, high-capacity hard disk, adequate expandability, and other features.

Today, laptops provide most (but not all) of the benefits of a desktop computer, while being light enough to carry virtually anywhere without problem. It is primarily these devices that have produced the revolution in "take-it-with-you" computing.

What Is a Laptop Computer?

Although there is no absolute definition of a laptop, most of these devices meet the following minimum criteria:

- An Intel 8086 or more powerful processor
- An integrated, flat-panel screen
- An integrated keyboard
- A weight of 8 to 15 pounds
- A hard disk
- At least one floppy disk drive
- At least one standard (ISA) expansion slot
- At least one parallel and one serial port

Along with laptops, other types of portable computing devices have come on the market. These include notebook and palmtop computers. Notebooks, as their name implies, are about the size of a writing tablet, usually no larger than 9 by 12 inches. They weigh from about 4 to 8 pounds and are about 1½ to 2½ inches thick. Notebooks provide less computing power than laptops but are easier to carry.

Palmtops are about the size of a desk calculator and provide maximum transportability while sacrificing even more capacity and performance than notebook computers. Palmtops do not offer touch-type keyboards and have very small screens. Most cannot run popular software applications and accessories. However, palmtops are useful for a number of low-level computing tasks, such as storing telephone numbers and addresses.

Although notebook and palmtop users will find much of the information in this book helpful, the material is primarily intended for laptop users. Within a few years, notebooks and palmtops will be more powerful, but for now, the laptop is the preferred method of computing on the road.

Also, non-DOS laptop computers do exist (Macintosh, for example), but they are not addressed in this book.

The Goal of this Guide

The goal of *The Laptop User's Survival Guide* is to make laptop users more comfortable, competent, and successful in working with their computers. Although desktop computers present their share of challenges, the nature of laptops combined with the perils of computing on the road add another level of complexity.

To help readers get the most from their laptops, each chapter in this guide presents specific tips that can be of benefit immediately. Where appropriate, we include the step-by-step actions for the approach being discussed.

Although the book can be used effectively by anyone with a laptop, readers that have at least some computer experience and a basic knowledge of MS-DOS commands will benefit the most. However, you do not have to be a computer expert to use this guide. Computer terms and concepts are explained when they are part of the discussion, and a glossary of terms is included as an appendix to the book.

An Overview of the Guide

The first 12 chapters of this book address typical needs of laptop users:

- Chapter 1, *Essential Battle Gear for Success,* provides suggestions for items to bring along with a laptop when you are traveling.

- Chapter 2, *Making the Most of Your Laptop Hardware,* describes methods for optimizing the performance of a laptop by increasing its random-access-memory capacity and using expansion slots appropriately.

- Chapter 3, *Managing Disk Space*, explains how to maximize hard disk space on a laptop.
- Chapter 4, *Exchanging Files on the Road*, offers suggestions for sharing files with other applications.
- Chapter 5, *Using Utility Packages to Avoid Disaster*, recommends utilities that are particularly valuable to laptop users.
- Chapter 6, *Printing on the Road*, includes information to help laptop users successfully produce output with unfamiliar printers.
- Chapter 7, *Laptop-to-Desktop File Transfer*, describes the use of file-transfer utilities to send and receive large amounts of data quickly and reliably.
- Chapter 8, *Effective Remote Communications*, explains how to configure a laptop for modem transmissions and how to optimize a modem's performance.
- Chapter 9, *Connecting Your Laptop to a Local Area Network*, provides tips for improving a laptop's networking capabilities.
- Chapter 10, *Faxing on the Road*, discusses the various types of faxing devices and how to use them while traveling.
- Chapter 11, *Working in Hostile Environments*, recommends strategies for working in motel rooms and airports and hooking up a modem to a nonstandard telephone line.
- Chapter 12, *Extra Tips for You and Your Laptop*, describes floppy disk drive compatibility issues, laptop battery power conservation, data backup while traveling, and information resources for laptop users who travel frequently.

The final chapter provides a reference guide to common commands in ten widely used software applications. The appendices also are references. Appendix A lists the products mentioned in this book along with the addresses and telephone numbers of the manufacturers. Appendix B is a glossary of the computer terms used in the book. Appendix C describes how to pare down your applications so that they are more portable.

The PopRef Disk Utility

The companion disk in the back of the book contains PopRef, a small, memory-resident help screen for DOS applications. When PopRef is resident, holding down a (user-assignable) hot key pops up a screen listing important function-key assignments and basic commands for the application you are running. Release the hot key, and the screen disappears, leaving you exactly where you were in the application. PopRef recognizes the half dozen or so most widely used applications and a few less common ones. It also includes a help screen applicable at the DOS command line. You'll find it very useful when you need a quick reminder of a function-key assignment or command in an unfamiliar application.

ONE

Essential Battle Gear for Success

The Laptop User's Survival Guide

Are you and your laptop computer ready for the trip out of home territory? The purchase of a laptop computer itself does not guarantee success while computing on the road. It has been our experience that many of the standard features associated with laptop computers will operate less than acceptably once outside the office or home. Described below are some key accessories that can enhance your laptop computer's performance on the road. See Appendix A for the names and addresses of equipment sources.

Longer Power Cords for Work Area Flexibility

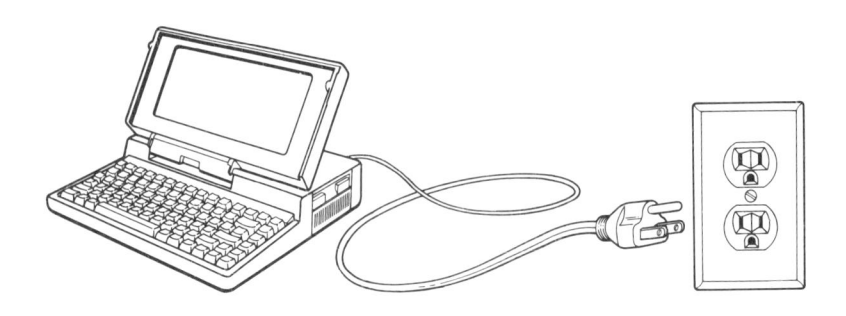

Even if you own a laptop computer that can run on a battery, one time or another, you will need to access an electrical outlet to perform your work or charge your batteries. The difference between a job or presentation being finished on time may come down to the length of your power cord. There will be many situations in which you will have little or no control over where you can use your laptop computer. You will be very disappointed when you find that an electrical outlet is out of your power cord's reach.

Essential Battle Gear for Success 3

BATTLE GEAR TIP #1: Bring a 12-Foot Power Cord

Bringing along a power cord that is longer than the one that came with the computer is highly beneficial for any laptop user. Most laptop computer manufacturers supply a 6-foot long power cord. We have found that a 12-foot power cord will generally provide the extra length you need. A power cord that is any longer will prove to be too cumbersome to use and an extra burden in terms of storage and increased weight.

Verify that the extra-length power cord will properly connect to your laptop computer. Connection schemes vary from device to device, and the standard plug may not work with your machine. The cost of a 12-foot power cord is around $4.50 (U.S.).

Although you could take an extension cord instead of a long power cord, using the wrong type of extension cord could ruin your laptop. Additionally, we have found that one long cord is easier to handle than two short ones. The cords can become disconnected, and their plugs get caught in table legs.

Improve Your Modem Capabilities with Longer Telephone Cables

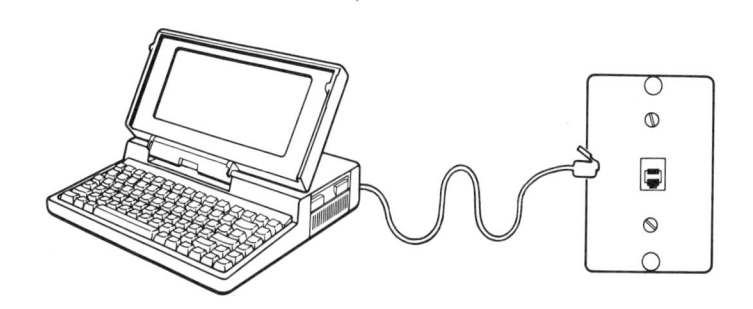

Communicating with other computers via modem is often necessary for laptop users. If the distance between your laptop computer's modem

and the nearest telephone jack exceeds the length of the telephone cable, you simply won't have the capability to access other computers.

BATTLE GEAR TIP #2: Bring a Long Phone Cable

Owning a telephone cable that is longer than the standard size will prevent many frustrating situations. Most modem manufacturers supply a telephone cable that is 7 feet long. We have found that a telephone cable of 15 to 25 feet in length is better suited for laptop computing communications. If your needs are even more demanding, self-recoiling telephone cables in lengths of 50 or 100 feet are available from most telephone supply stores.

When determining the most effective length of telephone cable for your laptop, consider the need for access to an electrical outlet (for your power cord) if you are not using a battery. In many cases, an electrical outlet is not located near a telephone jack. The cost of a 15-foot telephone cable is about $3.95 (U.S.).

If you do not have access to a telephone line with standard modular connectors, standard telephone cable will not work. See Chapter 11 for tips on how to handle this situation.

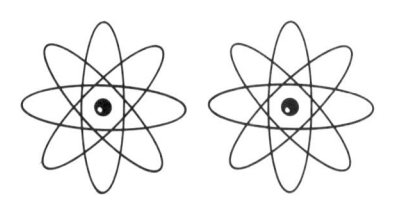

Bring Extra Battery Packs for an Additional Power Source

As a laptop computer user, you have probably found that there are never enough sources of power supply. No matter what type of battery

Essential Battle Gear for Success   5

configuration your laptop computer uses, it rarely can meet the long-term demands you may place on it.

BATTLE GEAR TIP #3: Double Your Power

To better harness the power of your laptop, it is a good idea to have twice the amount of battery life on hand than what you expect to use. You can downgrade your requirements if you have suitable access to an electrical outlet and a power cord that is long enough to reach it. See Chapter 12 for more information about how to manage the use of your laptop computer battery.

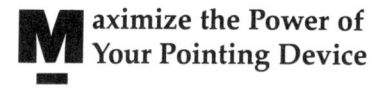

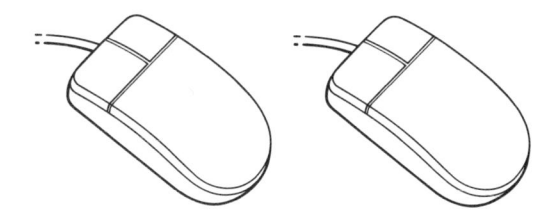

Maximize the Power of Your Pointing Device

The growth in popularity of the graphical user interface (GUI) has made the mouse (or other pointing device) critical to the performance of software applications. In an ideal computer world, there is always enough desktop space for a mouse and mouse pad. However, in many situations, work space for your pointing device may be nonexistent.

BATTLE GEAR TIP #4: Buy Another Pointing Device

If you have a mouse and use it with a desktop computer, keep that mouse attached to that computer and buy another pointing device. Why

6   The Laptop User's Survival Guide

spend the extra money on a second pointing device? One reason is that it eliminates the need to disconnect a mouse from one computer for use on your laptop. Not only does this approach save time, but it also avoids the frustration associated with forgetting to bring along a critical accessory.

The problem of limited work space for your mouse can be solved by purchasing a pointing device that can work on any level surface or will attach to your laptop computer.

One device that does not require desktop space is Logitech's TrackMan Portable mouse, which is illustrated in Figure 1.1. The TrackMan comes with a 2-foot cable and serial connector and attaches to the side of your laptop through a spring clamp. As you roll the trackball in the pointing device with your thumb, the screen pointer moves in the direction the ball is spinning. Along with the device, Logitech provides a software utility to improve mouse screen pointer visibility on poorly lit LCD screens.

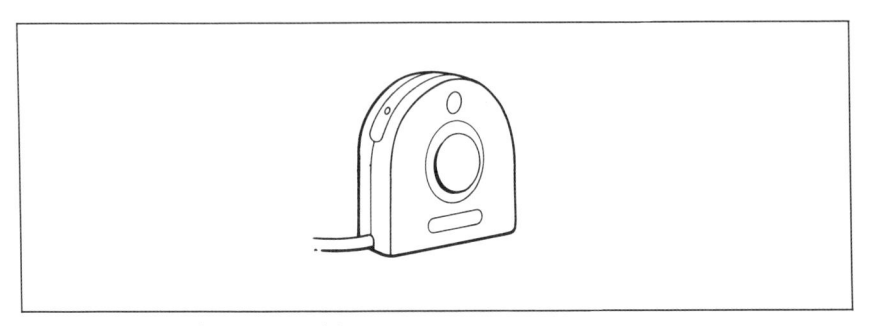

Figure 1.1: TrackMan Portable Mouse

Another pointing device that does not require desk space is the Microsoft Ballpoint Mouse, shown in Figure 1.2. The device contains a small ball that you spin to move the cursor. It can be clipped directly onto your laptop.

Essential Battle Gear for Success 7

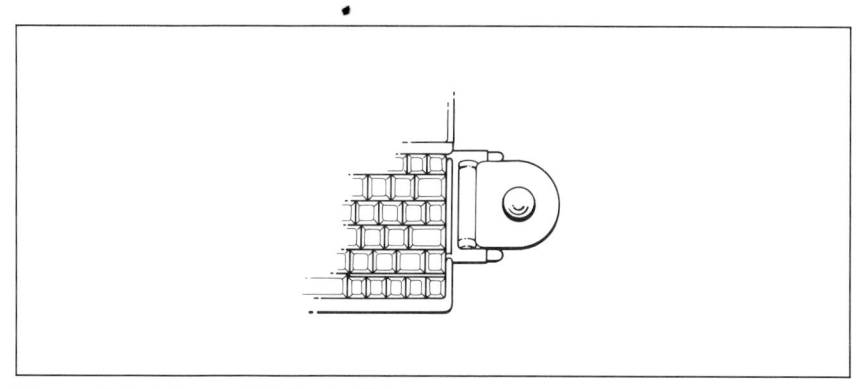

Figure 1.2: Microsoft Ballpoint Mouse

Fluent Communication with Multipurpose Modems

Your ability to get key information into other people's hands can often be tied to your laptop computer's ability to communicate with another computer, a bulletin board service, or a facsimile machine (fax). Years ago, having this kind of electronic communication capability while working on the road was nice but not required. In today's business environment, this capability is usually demanded.

BATTLE GEAR TIP #5: Get a Fax Modem

Having the ability to fax documents directly from your laptop is something that all laptop users should seriously consider. You can purchase fax devices as either fax only or as a combination fax and modem. Modems allow computers to connect with one another and exchange data that can then be manipulated; fax boards allow only sending and receiving images that cannot be manipulated by most applications. On the other hand, fax modems perform all the functions of a standard modem and also operate as a fax. There are some fax modems that just receive data, while others act as both sending and receiving devices. Since fax modems can

8 The Laptop User's Survival Guide

communicate as either a fax or a modem, they eliminate the need to purchase two separate devices.

Like standard modems, fax modems are available as small external devices. This means they provide the added benefit of not using an expansion card slot in your laptop computer. An internal fax-modem board, which must be installed in your laptop, is shown in Figure 1.3. An external fax-modem device, which plugs into the back of your laptop and connects to the telephone jack in the wall, is illustrated in Figure 1.4.

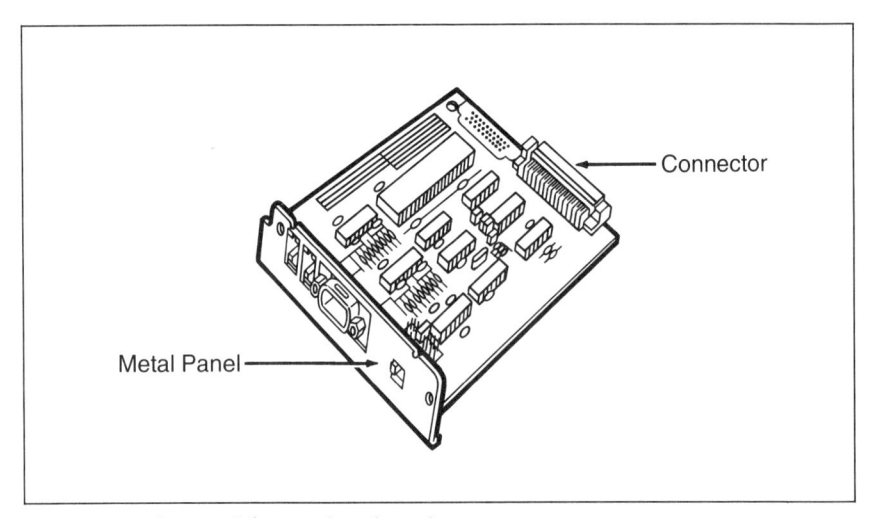

Figure 1.3: Internal fax-modem board

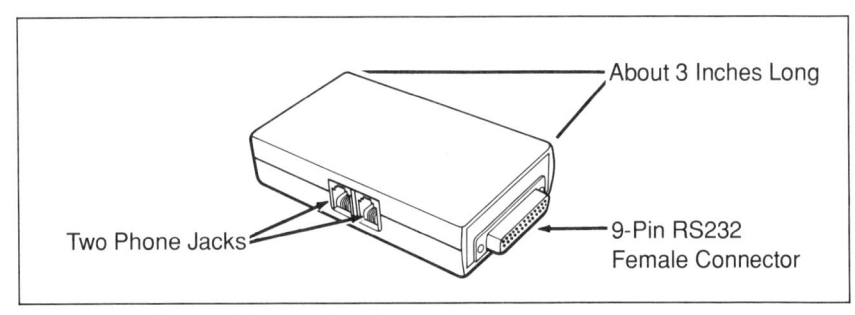

Figure 1.4: External fax-modem device

Essential Battle Gear for Success

See Chapter 8 for more information about faxing documents from your laptop.

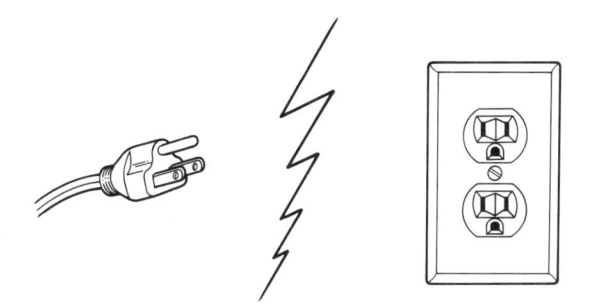

Quick Changes in Power Connections

There is still a great percentage of office buildings, homes, hotels, and motels that have not updated their electrical wiring. The possession of all the laptop gadgetry in the world may become inconsequential if you are not prepared for this situation.

BATTLE GEAR TIP #6: Bring a 3-to-2 Adapter

It has been our experience that the potential for trouble-free laptop computing is significantly strengthened by the possession of a 3-to-2 plug adapter. We say this with some caution because, technically speaking, the electrical line (and therefore your laptop if it is connected) is not properly grounded when using this approach. If your battery power is used up or nonexistent, and the demand for power outweighs the need for a proper ground, this inexpensive plug can be a lifesaver.

All Dressed Up and Nowhere to Print

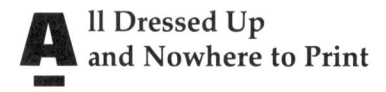

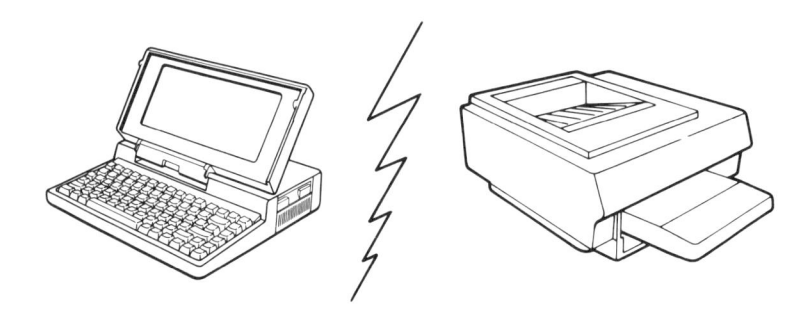

A document or presentation that does not need some last-minute editing or modification is the exception not the rule. For laptop computer users operating away from the home office, this means that the affected document will need to be printed again. All of your last-minute changes become worthless if your laptop computer cannot physically connect to a nearby printer.

BATTLE GEAR TIP #7: Take Printer Cables

We highly recommend that you store a set of printer cables with your laptop computer. At first glance, this tactic may appear to be of limited value, but in day-to-day operations, having printer cables (10 to 15 feet long) will prove to be most beneficial.

Disrupting an existing connection between a desktop computer and a printer will be cumbersome at best, and depending on company policy, may not even be allowed. Finding a set of unused printer cables can be time-consuming and frustrating. The best alternative is to have your own printer cables.

Originally, printers were manufactured to contain only one of the two major (serial and parallel) connection schemes. The introduction of AppleTalk (now LocalTalk) provided a third major connection scheme.

Today, some printer manufacturers, such as NEC, provide all three connection schemes as a standard feature. The most popular laser printer, the Hewlett-Packard LaserJet II, allows for connection to cables with connectors configured for either serial or parallel ports. Our personal choice is to carry a set of printer cables with parallel connectors because of the ease in configuration. See Chapter 6 for further information about printing on the road.

Eliminate the Floppy Disk Size Controversy

Although the phrase "industry standard" is popular in the personal computer field, it is not a label you can rely on. When it comes to how personal computers are configured, *industry* and *standard* become mutually exclusive terms. Floppy disks and their formatting capacities can be frustrating when you are trying to transfer data between computers. File transfer can be all but impossible if the floppy disk drives you wish to use have different sizes or capacities.

BATTLE GEAR TIP #8: Bring a Transfer Program and Cable

Having a file-transfer program and transfer cables on hand to make the exchange possible can save hours of time when you are trying to get data from one computer to another. This capability not only eliminates the floppy disk incompatibility issue, but it also avoids the problem of transferring files that are too big to be stored on one floppy disk and reduces the time needed to transfer a large number of files. See Chapters 4, 5, and 7 for more information about transferring files.

Take Advantage of a Network Connection

Personal computers attached to networks make up 8 million of the more than 50 million personal computers in the marketplace. The chances that you can benefit from connecting your laptop to a network are quite high if your work takes you to offices that have a personal computer network system.

Essential Battle Gear for Success   **13**

BATTLE GEAR TIP #9: Buy a Networking Device

If you frequently take your laptop to sites where networks are used, consider purchasing a network interface card or an external network adapter that will attach to one of your laptop computer's ports. Figure 1.5 illustrates an internal card, and Figure 1.6 shows an external adapter.

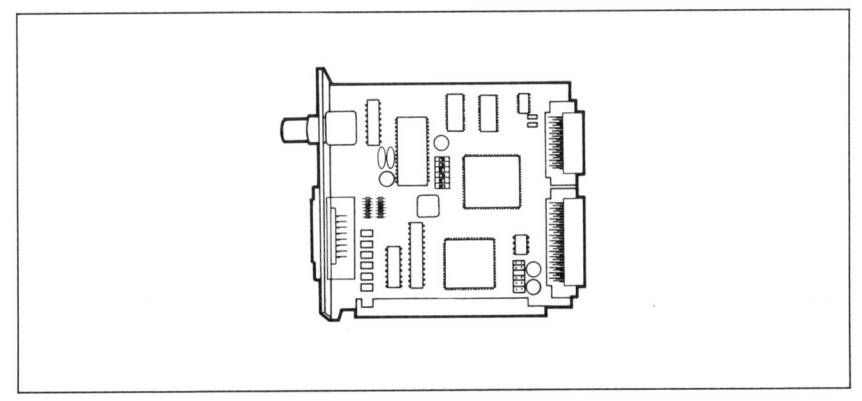

Figure 1.5: Internal network interface card

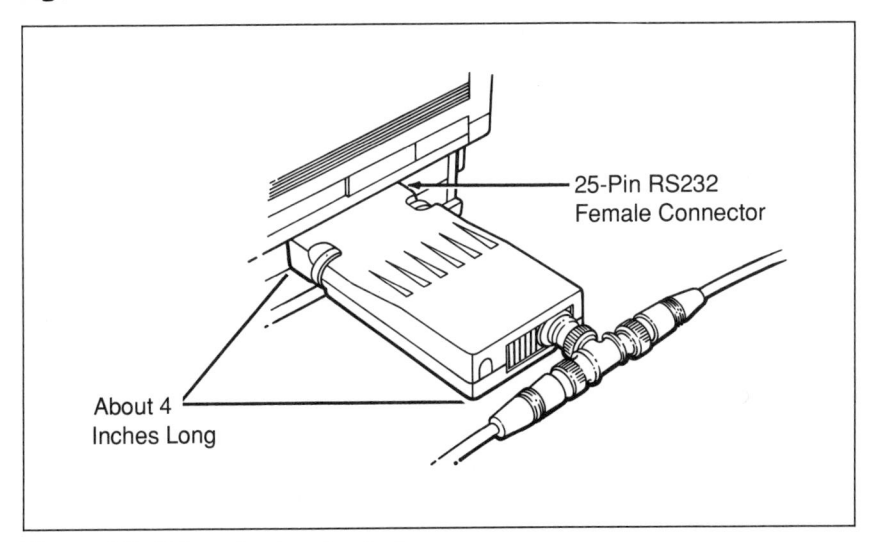

Figure 1.6: External network adapter

Depending on the type of network you are using, you may need an Ethernet or ARCnet card, as well as the appropriate device drivers and networking software to work on a Novell or LAN Manager network.

Owning a network connection device that can be used on one or more networks can eliminate the need for many of the accessories we suggested earlier, such as a fax modem and printer cable.

See Chapter 9 for more information about networking devices.

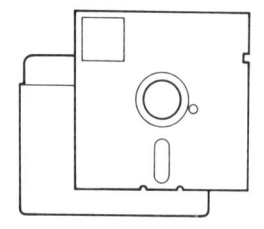

Keep Critical Programs and Files on Floppy Disks to Avoid Disaster

Being out on the road and having no backup copies of critical files and programs is similar to crossing 100 miles of desert on foot without water or food.

BATTLE GEAR TIP #10: Take Backup Copies

We highly recommend that you bring along copies of the master disks of essential programs. For example, MS-DOS, Windows (if you work in that environment), and your word processing program would be wise choices if you are going to travel far away from the office for an extended period of time. This will avoid panic on your part when (not if) your laptop computer fails and a file becomes corrupted or is inadvertently deleted.

Making a Case for Cases

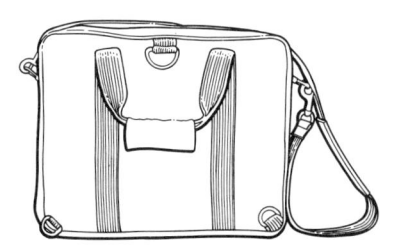

Most laptop computer manufacturers provide a carrying case either as a standard feature or as an option. Normally, these cases supply space to store the laptop computer itself and a limited amount of accessories.

BATTLE GEAR TIP #11: Put It All in a Case

If you want to take along all the battle gear we have noted, we recommend that you look for a storage case that provides the proper amount of room. There are many third-party manufacturers of laptop computer cases. Cases are priced from $100 to $300 and can store up to 50 pounds of equipment.

Sort Out What You Really Need

Although we think each of our tips is important, the combined weight of all the accessories we have identified may be more than the weight of your laptop computer. Be judicious in the selection of the components you really need and the items that will provide the most benefit. For example, many laptop users have no access to a printer but need printing capability. This situation requires that you bring along a printer.

We have found that planning what to take is an ongoing process rather than a one-time decision. For most trips, we try to discover what ground rules will apply where we will be working. If there are no clear definitions of what the work environment will be or which tools will be available, we recommend that you take along every item that could be necessary for you to complete your task.

Battle Gear Check List

Here is a check list of all the items mentioned in this chapter:

- Longer power cords
- Longer telephone cable
- Extra battery pack
- Pointing device
- Fax or fax-modem board
- 3-to-2 plug adapter
- Longer printer cable
- File-transfer utility
- Network adapter
- Backup copies of master files and applications on floppy disk
- Carrying case

Remember, you probably will not need to take all the items, and your requirements may vary with your destination. See Appendix A for specific battle gear sources.

TWO

Making the Most of Your Laptop Hardware

Since space is limited within the chassis of a laptop, it generally has less room for everything. Unless you spend a great deal of money, laptops simply cannot contain the same hardware that is within most desktop units. Despite this constraint, laptop users make the mistake of assuming that they can do everything a desktop user can. This chapter considers these constraints and provides tips for making your laptop work more like a desktop.

Your Laptop's Environment

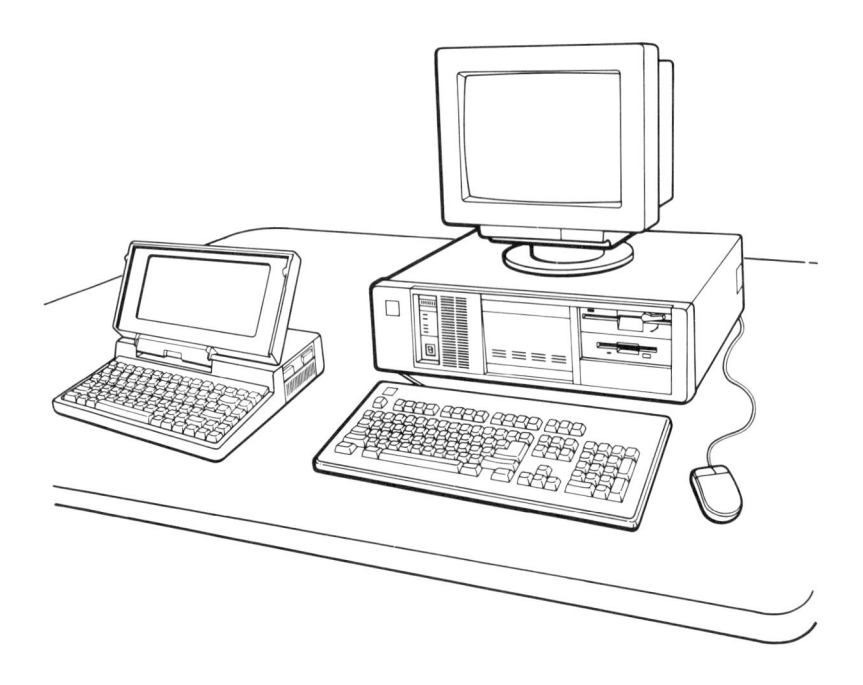

Your laptop's "environment" consists of all its various hardware and software components. For the most part, it is the same environment as

Making the Most of Your Laptop Hardware

that found in your desktop computer. Both run the MS-DOS operating system (and sometimes Windows); both run the same kinds of application software; and both have memory, disk drives, a central processing unit (CPU), and other components. However, despite the overwhelming number of similarities, laptops are different because of the design and manufacturing constraints inherent in producing a smaller computer with a flat-panel screen that must run on direct-current (battery) power. These differences include the following:

- Laptops typically support less random-access memory (RAM) than desktops. While many desktops support up to 8 megabytes (MB) of RAM on the motherboard (the board on which the CPU resides), most laptops support only 4MB. Although you can add more RAM to a laptop (usually an additional 4MB), this requires the use of an expansion slot, which you will want to reserve for something other than RAM.

- Although desktop computers have up to eight expansion slots through which you can add fax-modem boards, additional ports, network interfaces, and other capabilities, most laptops have three or fewer expansion slots. This is a critical constraint that can limit the power and flexibility of your laptop.

- Laptops are generally equipped with different monitors than desktops. Most newer laptops come with monochrome higher resolution VGA-compatible screens, but older laptops have the lower resolution CGA and EGA video standards. With a desktop, you can trade in your monitor for a better one and buy a new video board to support it, but a laptop screen is permanently built in, meaning that you must make the most of it or use an external (and nonportable) VGA desktop monitor.

Although these inherent laptop constraints can pose problems, there are a variety of things you can do to avoid them. Some solutions are presented in the following sections.

Increase Your RAM Capacity

RAM typically presents greater problems in a laptop than in a desktop. If you run the same applications on your laptop that you run on your desktop, you will need sufficient RAM for both machines. Figure 2.1 diagrams how your computer system uses memory.

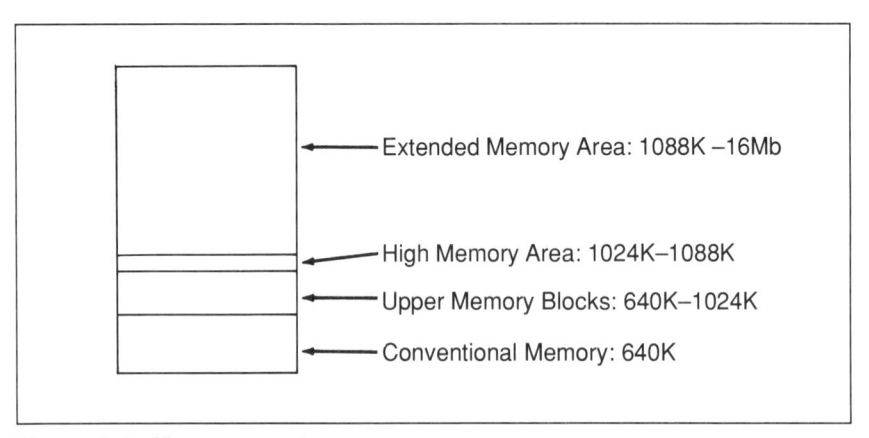

```
┌─────────────────────────────────────────────────┐
│   ┌─────────────┐                               │
│   │             │                               │
│   │             │◄──── Extended Memory Area: 1088K –16Mb
│   │             │                               │
│   │             │                               │
│   ├─────────────┤◄──── High Memory Area: 1024K–1088K
│   ├─────────────┤◄──── Upper Memory Blocks: 640K–1024K
│   │             │◄──── Conventional Memory: 640K
│   └─────────────┘                               │
└─────────────────────────────────────────────────┘
```

Figure 2.1: How your system uses memory

The major consideration for a laptop is having enough memory to run MS-DOS applications, regardless of whether you run them in the Windows environment. When running in enhanced mode, Windows 3.0 gives you "multiple virtual MS-DOS machines" or, in other words, the ability to run several MS-DOS applications in different windows on your screen simultaneously.

Although Windows can use many megabytes of RAM in the form of extended memory, it does not give your computer more memory to run MS-DOS applications because these applications still run in conventional memory, which is 640 kilobytes (K) of RAM. In fact, loading Windows actually takes away about 20K of conventional RAM from each of your MS-DOS applications. To run Windows and Windows applications, you

Making the Most of Your Laptop Hardware

will need a bare minimum of 2MB; 4MB is the recommended amount for Windows 3.0 enhanced mode. The following tips should help give you some additional RAM for your MS-DOS applications.

RAM TIP #1: Use a Memory Manager for Additional Memory

If you have a version of MS-DOS earlier than release 5.0, you should definitely consider upgrading your laptop to this new version. MS-DOS 5.0 includes a memory manager (as well as many other new features) and makes available an additional 45K of conventional RAM. If you run Windows 3.0 in enhanced mode, MS-DOS 5.0 provides an additional 45K of RAM for each MS-DOS application that you run under Windows.

If you do not want to upgrade to MS-DOS 5.0, we recommend that you get a memory manager program such as Quarterdeck's QEMM. QEMM frees additional memory for MS-DOS applications by loading system drivers (such as those for local area networks) into upper memory above the 640K boundary.

Figure 2.2 illustrates how your laptop's conventional and upper memory can be managed.

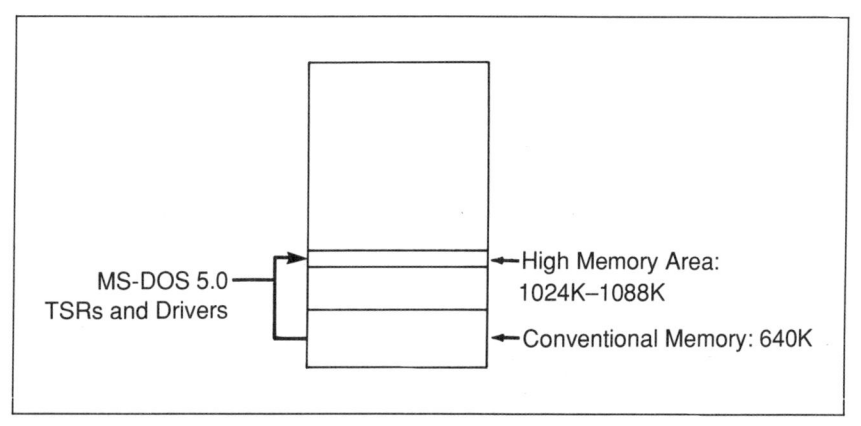

Figure 2.2: Loading programs into upper memory

RAM TIP #2: Remove Unnecessary Device Drivers

At your office, you probably use your laptop in a different way than you do on the road. Some drivers that you normally load at your office can be omitted from your CONFIG.SYS file in order to obtain more free RAM for your applications while on the road. Two primary examples are network and video drivers.

If you attach your laptop to a network or an external monitor at your office, you may want to prevent these drivers from loading while you are traveling. Simply edit your CONFIG.SYS file (with EDLIN or a full-screen text editor such as Microsoft Word) and place the letters *REM* in front of your network or video drivers.

Figure 2.3 shows an example of a modified CONFIG.SYS file. Notice that REM has been added before the LAN Manager drivers and also before a special driver (XANSI.SYS) that the Orchid Pro Designer II video board uses.

```
FILES = 20
BUFFERS = 30
DEVICE=C:\HIMEM.SYS
DEVICE=C:\SMARTDRV.SYS
REM DEVICE=C:\PROE\XANSI.SYS
LASTDRIVE=Z
REM DEVICE=C:\LANMAN.DOS\DRIVERS\PROTMAN\PROTMAN.DOS
/i:C:\LANMAN.DOS
REM DEVICE=C:\LANMAN.DOS\DRIVERS\ETHERNET\ELNKII\ELNKII.DOS
REM DEVICE=C:\LANMAN.DOS\DRIVERS\PROTOCOL\NETBEUI\NETBEUI.DOS
```

Figure 2.3: Sample CONFIG.SYS file modified to prevent video and network drivers from loading

Before you modify your CONFIG.SYS file, however, be sure to consult your network and video documentation to identify the names of the drivers that can be removed.

When you get back to your office, you can restore the drivers. Simply delete the letters *REM* and reboot your system to have the drivers loaded.

Alternatively, you can create a DOS *batch file* that switches you between two separate system configurations. Each system configuration— one for the office and one for the road—is specified by its own unique

Making the Most of Your Laptop Hardware

AUTOEXEC.BAT and CONFIG.SYS files. Your batch file copies the original two system files to different names, such as AUTOEXEC.ORG (ORG stands for original) and CONFIG.ORG, and renames the new ones to AUTOEXEC.BAT and CONFIG.SYS. By taking this approach, you can optimize how your laptop performs, reducing system hangups when you are away from the office. See your MS-DOS manual for details on creating batch files and system files.

In the examples shown in Figure 2.4, four batch files and two configuration files have been created to set up the office and road environments for a laptop. The batch file named OFFICE.BAT sets up the laptop for optimal use in an office environment, while the batch file ROAD.BAT sets up the laptop for optimal use on the road. Note that these are sample files only and are not intended to replace the ones on your system.

To execute a batch file, simply type in the first part of the name (such as OFFICE or ROAD) at the DOS command prompt and press the Enter key. You will need to reboot your system each time you execute one of these batch files; otherwise, DOS will not read the new AUTOEXEC.BAT and CONFIG.SYS system files.

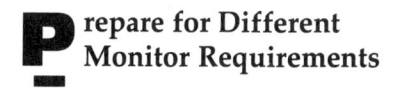

Prepare for Different Monitor Requirements

24 The Laptop User's Survival Guide

```
OFFICE.BAT: Batch file for switching to an office computing
environment

Copy C:\AUTOEXEC.OFF  C:\AUTOEXEC.BAT
Copy C:\CONFIG.OFF    C:\CONFIG.SYS

ROAD.BAT: Batch file for switching to a road computing
environment

Copy C:\AUTOEXEC.RD   C:\AUTOEXEC.BAT
Copy C:\CONFIG.RD     C:\CONFIG.SYS

AUTOEXEC.RD

REM ***Autoexec.bat for the road
PATH=C:\;C:\DOS;C:\WIN30;C:\PKZIP;C:\PCTOOLS
ECHO OFF
VER
PROMPT $P$G

SET TEMP=C:\WIN30\TEMP
REM *** TAKE OUT BATCH FILE TO START NETWORK
REM C:\NETWORK\NETWORK.BAT

CONFIG.RD

REM *** Config.sys for the road
REM *** LOWER THE AMOUNT OF FILES THAT CAN BE OPENED
FILES=25
BUFFERS=15
REM *** REMOVE SHELL AND SCANNER DRIVER FROM LOADING
REM SHELL= C:\COMMAND.COM /e:512 /p
REM DEVICE=C:\DOS\SJDRIVER.SYS
DEVICE =C:\HIMEM.SYS
DEVICE=C:\WIN30\SMARTDRV.SYS 2048 512

AUTOEXEC.OFF

REM *** Autoexec.bat for the office
PATH=C:\;C:\DOS;C:\WIN30;C:\PKZIP;C:\PCTOOLS
ECHO OFF
VER

PROMPT $P$G
SET TEMP=C:\WIN30\TEMP
C:\NETWORK\NETWORK.BAT

CONFIG.RD
```

Figure 2.4: Sample batch and configuration files for different office and road environments

Making the Most of Your Laptop Hardware

```
FILES=40
BUFFERS=15
SHELL= C:\COMMAND.COM /e:512 /p
DEVICE=C:\DOS\SJDRIVER.SYS
DEVICE =C:\HIMEM.SYS
DEVICE=C:\WIN30\SMARTDRV.SYS 2048 512
```

Figure 2.4: Sample batch and configuration files for different office and road environments (cont'd)

Most of the newer laptops are equipped with at least VGA-quality (640 × 480 resolution) monitors. However, there are a large number of older laptops that have only an EGA or a CGA monitor. Many veteran laptop users have a smart strategy of making VGA monitors available to them at their destinations (perhaps a field office of their corporation).

Since many laptops support an external monitor port, they can readily be attached to VGA screens and run VGA-quality applications such as Windows. In locations where access to VGA is not available (such as in an airplane), use DOS character-based applications since EGA and CGA are not suitable for running VGA-quality applications.

MONITOR TIP #1: Be Ready for VGA

If you have a laptop with a CGA or EGA monitor and you want to attach it to a VGA monitor, you will need the proper hardware and drivers.

Most laptops have their monitor hardware built onto the motherboard. Make sure that this hardware supports VGA output. If it does not, you will have to install a VGA-capable monitor board in your laptop. Ask your laptop manufacturer to recommend a board. Many laptops will not support standard desktop monitor boards.

Also, make sure that you have the appropriate cable—one that matches your laptop's monitor connector—available at your destination site. Otherwise, take a cable with you.

If you want to use Windows, you will need to run the Windows Setup program (usually an icon located in the Main group on your screen) to change your display option to VGA. Make sure that you bring copies of your Windows master disks with you, because you may not have the

Windows VGA drivers loaded in your Windows System subdirectory (C:WINDOWSSYSTEM) on your laptop. Once you select VGA (or other appropriate VGA-style driver), Windows will ask you to insert one of the Windows master disk copies to install the requested driver and then restart Windows so that your changes can take effect. Once this VGA driver is loaded onto your hard disk, it stays there permanently, and you will not have to run Windows Setup again to install it.

If you are not running Windows but have MS-DOS applications that support VGA mode, make sure that you have the individual application VGA drivers (if needed) available on your hard disk.

Use Expansion Slots Wisely

For obvious reasons, laptops are designed to be as small as possible. One of the consequences of their small size is the lack of expansion slots. Although desktops typically come with up to eight expansion slots, laptops usually come with only two or three. Fortunately, laptop manufacturers build many features into the motherboard of the laptop itself. For example, some laptops incorporate modems into a proprietary slot and build video circuitry directly on the motherboard, whereas desktops often require the use of two standard expansion slots for these items. Figure 2.5 shows a typical laptop slot configuration.

EXPANSION SLOT TIP #1: Use Slots for Fax, Modem, or Network Board

Since your laptop has a limited number of expansion slots, you must fill them wisely. For laptops, these are your usual choices:

- A modem (if not already installed in a proprietary slot)
- A fax board
- A combination fax-modem board

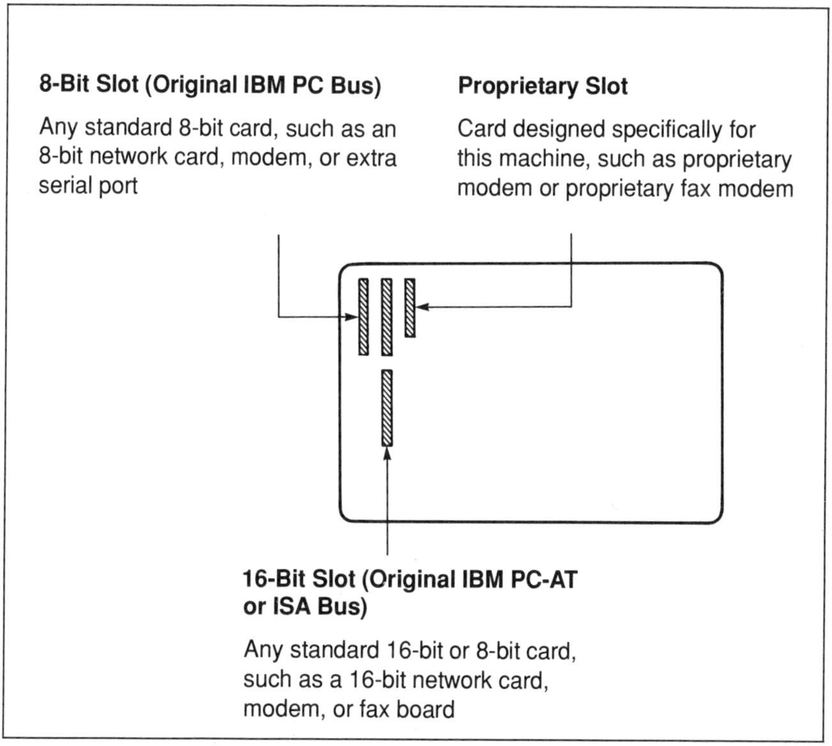

Making the Most of Your Laptop Hardware 27

8-Bit Slot (Original IBM PC Bus)

Any standard 8-bit card, such as an 8-bit network card, modem, or extra serial port

Proprietary Slot

Card designed specifically for this machine, such as proprietary modem or proprietary fax modem

16-Bit Slot (Original IBM PC-AT or ISA Bus)

Any standard 16-bit or 8-bit card, such as a 16-bit network card, modem, or fax board

Figure 2.5: A typical laptop slot configuration

- Extra memory
- A network board
- External video monitor board
- Tape backup

We recommend that you use internal expansion slots only for the items you will use the most often or that cannot be attached any other way. For example, internal slots should be used for items such as additional RAM or a super VGA video card.

Buy internal expansion boards only if you cannot purchase the capability as an external option. For example, before you purchase an internal fax board, investigate the possibility of purchasing an external "pocket fax" that plugs into the RS232 port of your laptop. This will save a critical expansion slot that you may need later. Do the same for backup devices and network boards—these are available in external form as well.

To optimize your expansion slot use, look for boards that combine two or more capabilities on a single board, even though they may be more expensive. For example, although boards that support both fax and modem capabilities can be somewhat costly, they are worth the extra money to save the slot that you would otherwise use with two separate boards.

THREE

Managing Disk Space

Since laptop manufacturing costs are already high, large-capacity disk drives (which are expensive) are typically not purchased with laptops. In fact, laptops average about half the hard-disk capacity of comparable desktops, typically between 20MB and 80MB.

If you load MS-DOS and four software packages, such as Microsoft Windows 3.0, Lotus 1-2-3, PC Tools, and Crosstalk for Windows, you've already taken about 14MB of disk space. And, of course, this does not include your user files. It follows that one of the most frequent problems encountered by laptop owners is running out of disk space—often at a critical moment.

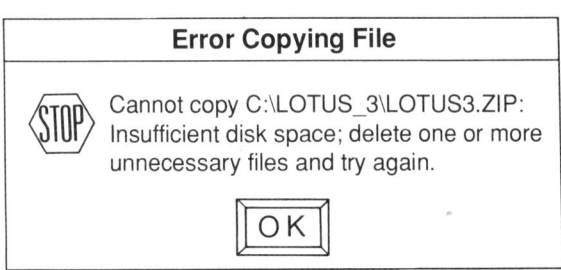

Maximizing Your Hard Disk Space

> **Error Copying File**
>
> Cannot copy C:\LOTUS_3\LOTUS3.ZIP: Insufficient disk space; delete one or more unnecessary files and try again.
>
> [O K]

What most laptop owners (and even desktop owners) don't know is that their current use of hard disk space is as much as 60 percent inefficient. It is not unusual, for example, to have a full 40MB disk with as much as 24MB of space that could be free if a few simple steps were taken. The following tips should save you at least a few megabytes.

HARD DISK TIP #1: Compress Files with the Save As Command

Perhaps you have seen a directory listing of your user files and wondered why they are so large. For example, a Word document consisting of 10,000 characters may somehow appear on your disk as a file of 18,000 bytes. Since a character takes a single byte of space, what occupies the

Managing Disk Space 31

extra 8000 bytes? Some of this extra space is consumed by special formatting characters, which indicate character styles (such as bold or italic), the document's margins, font specifications, and other characteristics. However, a great deal of this space is taken up by old edits that you made to the file.

Some applications do not delete old edits when you save or close a file. The result is that files gradually grow, sometimes to two or three times their original size. This problem can be especially severe with applications such as PageMaker that create large files. You should try using the Save As option in each of your applications in order to purge all your old edits from your files. Respond Yes if you are asked if you want to replace the old version (you can keep the same file name). Then check to see if your files are actually smaller.

If your application does not have a Save As command, select the command that saves the file under a different file name, and then delete the old version. Depending on how old your files are and how many changes you have made to them, you can compress an entire directory to about 50 percent of its former size.

HARD DISK TIP #2: Remove Unnecessary Files

Remove files that you never use, especially user files that have been sitting in your directories for months. Just in case, however, store some of the ones that you feel might be useful on floppy disks. If your laptop has a floppy disk drive that can read 3½-inch, high-density disks (which can store more information than 5¼-inch disks), you will not have to take that many floppy disks with you.

In addition to your user files, storing the following DOS System files on floppy disks instead of on your hard disk can free several megabytes of space:

FDISK.EXE	60K	Used for formatting and partitioning hard disks
SELECT.*	60K	Used to install DOS
EMM386.SYS	87K	Remove only if you never load this driver from CONFIG.SYS

32 The Laptop User's Survival Guide

GWBASIC.EXE	80K	Remove only if you never do BASIC programming
LINK.EXE	44K	Used for programming tasks
SHELL.*	230K	Remove only if you do not use the DOS Shell (version 4.01 or higher)
DEBUG.COM	21K	Used for programming tasks
NLSFUNC.EXE	7K	Remove only if you do not use foreign-language support
SHARE.EXE	13K	Remove only if you will not connect to a network
Total	**515K**	

These files are usually stored in a directory named \DOS (or something very similar).

If you use Windows, you can also store the following Windows System files on floppy disks:

EMM386.SYS	60K	Remove only if this driver does not appear in CONFIG.SYS
*.BMP	242K	Remove if you do not use the desktop background bit-maps
PBRUSH.*	230K	Windows Paintbrush application
RECORDER.*	80K	Windows Recorder accessory
REVERSI.EXE	6K	Windows Reversi game
SOL.EXE	181K	Windows Solitaire game
Total	**799K**	

These files may be found in the Windows directory (usually called \Windows or \Win30) on your hard disk.

Removing other Windows applications such as CALENDAR.EXE, CALC.EXE, and WRITE.EXE, will free additional hard-disk space, but make sure to take the floppy disk copies with you so that you will have the calendar, calculator, and word processor if you need them. The Windows Write application can be especially useful for importing and exporting text to and from Windows applications. Even if you do not remove any Windows files, make sure to take the Windows disks with you just in case you need to reinstall Windows from scratch.

Additionally, many applications come with unnecessary files (such as demo files) that can be removed. Excel for Windows, for example, comes with over 360K of demo files that you can do without.

Using Utilities to Defragment and Compress Files

There are many utilities designed to help you maximize your hard-disk space. These are categorized as defragmentation and compression utilities.

DISK UTILITY TIP #1: Use a Defragmentation Utility

Whether you are a laptop or desktop user, your hard disk eventually suffers from fragmentation. When you use a freshly formatted disk, all the information in your files is initially placed on the disk in contiguous fashion, which means that each piece of data in a file (byte) is physically next to another piece of information in that same file. As the disk fills up, the operating system finds it more difficult to pack this data together efficiently. The result is that the information on the disk becomes scattered, leaving "holes," or wasted disk areas that hold no data.

A number of defragmentation utilities are available to help you recover some of this lost space. PC Tools Deluxe is a good example. If you are removing files as recommended in the preceding hard-disk tip, be sure to do this before using a defragmentation utility, because removing unnecessary files will enable greater compacting to take place.

Although you may not always recover unused space when you defragment your disk, you will make the disk's overall storage space more efficient, as well as speed up your file-access time.

As a general rule, never run a defragmentation utility from within Windows (unless the utility is written for use with Windows) and be sure to disable all disk managers and disk-caching devices before doing so. See Chapter 5 for more information about defragmentation utilities.

DISK UTILITY TIP #2: Compress and Archive Selected Files

If you don't think you will be using certain files while on your trip, use a compression utility such as PKZIP to compress these files and store them in an archive file on your disk. You can use a utility to compress any files, including document, application, and text files. See Chapter 5 for more information about compression utilities.

After installing PKZIP, to compress your files, first change to the directory where your application resides (*directory name*) with the following command:

CD *directory name*

and press Enter. Then type the command to compress all files in that directory and store them in an archive file (*archivename*):

PKZIP -a *.* *archivename*

and press Enter.

To display a list of options you can use with PKZIP, type the following command:

PKZIP

and press Enter.

You can save much more space by following all the other tips presented in this chapter (use the Save As option, remove unnecessary files, and use a defragmentation utility) before compressing your files. If you do not, you will be compressing space that should not be there in the first place.

Managing Your Windows Swap File

When it comes to software, few programs can take as much space on your hard disk as Windows 3.0. Although the Windows directory itself is not that big (about 2MB), running Windows 3.0 in enhanced mode can take an additional 5MB or more, depending on how you have your swap file set up.

SWAP FILE TIP #1: Adjust the Size of Your Windows 3.0 Swap File

A *swap file* is an area of your hard disk that Windows uses as a substitute for RAM if it runs out of RAM. This is also known as *virtual memory*. Although slower than RAM, it can make your system seem as if it has unlimited extended memory. This feature is available only to Windows users with at least an 80386SX-based system.

There are three kinds of swap files: temporary, permanent, and application. A temporary swap file is created when you start Windows in enhanced mode if you have not already set up a permanent swap file. This file is named WIN386.SWP and is normally located in your Windows directory. The file will be deleted when you exit Windows. A swap file makes entering and exiting Windows slower, but it does not take away storage space for other applications when you are not running Windows.

Permanent swap files remain on your disk permanently and thus take away hard-disk space that could otherwise be used for storage. If you run Windows most of the time, then a small permanent swap file on your laptop's hard disk will provide you with extra virtual memory. If you run Windows less than 50 percent of the time, a temporary swap file is the best solution.

Run the Windows Setup program to see if you have a permanent swap file. You will see a Setup box similar to the one shown in Figure 3.1.

```
┌─────────────────────────────────────────────────────────┐
│  ─              Windows Setup                        ▼  │
│  Options  Help                                          │
│                                                         │
│  Display:      VGA                                      │
│  Keyboard:     Enhanced 101 or 102 key US and Non US    │
│  Mouse:        Microsoft, or IBM PS/2                   │
│  Network:      Novell Netware 2.10 or above, or Novell  │
│  ─────────────────────────────────────────────────────  │
│  Swap file:    None                                     │
│                                                         │
└─────────────────────────────────────────────────────────┘
```

Figure 3.1: Viewing your swap file type

You can create a permanent swap file or modify the size of an existing one by starting Windows in real mode, with the command Win/r, and running the Swapfile program (SWAPFILE.EXE). You will see the Swapfile box, which will look something like the one shown in Figure 3.2. (See the Windows user's manual for more information about running the Swapfile program.)

```
┌─────────────────────────────────────────────────────────┐
│                     Swapfile                            │
│  Swapfile has found a suitable location for a swap file │
│  on drive C:                                  [ Create ]│
│                                                         │
│    Largest possible swap file size:  2696K bytes        │
│    Total free disk space:           13128K bytes [Next Drive]│
│                                                         │
│                                               [ Cancel ]│
│    Recommended swap file size:  [2696]▲▼ K bytes        │
│                                               [ Help... ]│
└─────────────────────────────────────────────────────────┘
```

Figure 3.2: Starting the Windows Swapfile program

A permanent swap file consists of two hidden, write-protected files, named SPART.PAR and 386SPART.PAR. These files should never be deleted, moved, or renamed by a means other than through the Swapfile program.

An *application* swap file is created and used when you start a non-Windows application and are running Windows in real or standard mode. These files are hidden, and their names start with the characters *WOA*. At least 512K of hard-disk RAM is required for an application swap file. The more free hard-disk space available for Windows, the more non-Windows applications you can run at one time.

If, after implementing all the suggestions presented here, you still have only a few megabytes left on your disk, you can take the drastic step of removing applications that you think you won't need from your hard disk and take them with you on floppy disks. Unfortunately, if you have reached this point, it is time to upgrade to a larger hard disk, because installing and deinstalling applications is not only time-consuming but can create problems.

FOUR

Exchanging Files on the Road

Sooner or later, most laptop owners need to exchange files with other laptop or desktop computer users. But because of the large number of applications, each with its own file format, this job can be difficult or impossible. For example, suppose you travel to your destination only to discover that the people you meet with have WordPerfect 5.1, Lotus 1-2-3, and Ventura Publisher on their machine, while you have brought Word for Windows, Excel 2.1c, and PageMaker? How will you be able to share files?

Using the tips described in this chapter will increase your chances for smooth file transfer.

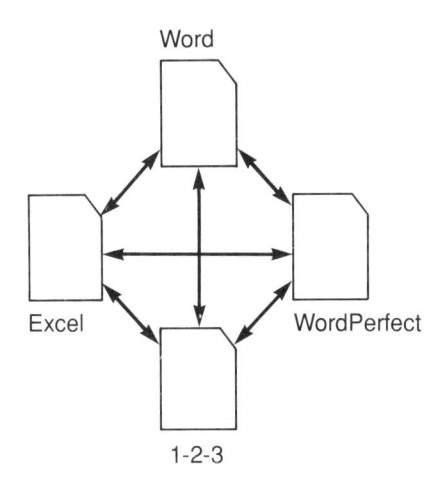

Sharing Files with Other Applications

```
                    Word
                     │
                     ↕
        Excel ←─────┼─────→ WordPerfect
                     ↕
                     │
                    1-2-3
```

Generally, files consist of either application-specific data or neutral data. *Application-specific* data is information that is meant to be understood by a single application. In other words, the information is "native" to that application. For example, an Excel spreadsheet file contains not just

Exchanging Files on the Road

user-supplied numbers, but also a wide range of other information concerning how that data is to be displayed and manipulated. This information is understood only by Excel.

Neutral data is information that is not specific to a single application. For example, the ASCII, TIFF, RTF, and Encapsulated PostScript formats are all neutral data formats. Each one of these contains its own level of formatting capabilities. ASCII format contains a very minimal level of formatting information (mostly tabs and carriage returns). RTF format has a much more robust set of formatting features, including different type styles and line spacing.

Most major applications provide for the exchange of data in either application-specific format or neutral format. This is accomplished through *filters*, which are utilities built into the application to provide conversion between its own internal format and some other file format.

Filters can work with either application-specific data or neutral data. For example, Microsoft Word has a filter that converts WordPerfect files (including all their formatting such as bold, italic, underlining, and margins) to their equivalent Word characteristics (and vice versa). Word also has a filter that converts ASCII format to and from Word format.

Application-specific filters are an excellent means of exchanging information because they preserve formatting characteristics, but no single application can include filters for every other application. In cases where applications do not support the particular filter necessary to exchange application-specific data, neutral format data filters, which do not retain the file's formatting features, must be used.

Importing File Information

Generally, information is imported and exported between applications. *Importing* information usually means that you are taking a different file format and converting it to your application's native format. However, it may also mean that a neutral file format such as TIFF is being placed (or embedded) within the document without being converted to a native format.

Applications vary in their method of importing information. Different applications have various commands for importing information, each of which may function differently.

To import data from another application into a given application, follow these steps:

1. Transfer the file that you want to import to the computer on which the importing application resides. (See Chapter 8 for more information about remote communications if you have trouble transferring the file.)

2. Launch the application that is to import the file (we'll call this the *importing application*). For example, if you want to import a WordPerfect file into Word, launch the Word application. (WordPerfect is the *exporting application*.)

3. Issue the command that the application uses to import files (such as Open, Place, or Import) and specify the file name of the file you wish to import. If the exporting application saved the file in the importing application's native format, the file should open without problems. If the file was saved in a nonnative (but supported) format, the application will do one of the following (consult your application's documentation for details):

   - Ask if you want to convert the file to the native format.
   - Ask you to specify the format which is being imported.
   - Identify the file's format and automatically convert it to the native format without prompting you.

If the application cannot import the file, this may mean that it does not have the appropriate filter to import the data. The only option at this point is to use the exporting application to save the file in a different format—one that can be recognized by the importing application. In most cases, you can export the information in ASCII format (unless it is a graphics file), as explained in the next section.

Exporting Data to Another Application

Exporting information usually means that you are taking your application's native format and converting it to a different format for use by a different application. To export data from an application for use in another application, follow these steps:

1. Launch the application from which you are exporting the file (the exporting application).

2. Open the file that you want to export to another application.

3. Select Save As (or the application's equivalent command) and find the file format options under which you can save the file. (Consult your application's documentation and learn how to save the file in a nonnative format before you go on the road.)

4. Select a format that the importing application supports and save the file under that format.

FILE SHARING TIP #1:
Use Applications that Support Standard Formats

The most popular file exchange formats, grouped by functional category, are listed in Table 4.1. If you plan to exchange files with other computer users, your applications should support a good selection of these formats. An application that cannot import or export a fairly wide range of file formats will eventually cause frustration.

Table 4.1: Standard Document Exchange Formats

Function	Format
Word Processing	
	Word for DOS (.DOC file extension)
	Word for Windows (.DOC file extension)
	WordPerfect for DOS (.WP5 file extension)
	WordStar (.WS file extension)
	Windows Write (.WRI file extension)
	Ami and Ami Professional (.SAM format)
	Text (unformatted characters, often referred to as ASCII text)
	DCA (Document Content Architecture)
	RTF (Rich Text Format)
	RFT (Revisable Form Text)
Graphic	
	PCX (PC Paintbrush, .PCX file extension)
	TIFF (Tagged Image File Format)
	Windows Paintbrush (.BMP file extension)
	PICT (Macintosh graphics format)
	EPS (Encapsulated PostScript)
	DRW (Micrographix)
	CGM (Computer Graphics Metafile, .CGM file extension, used by Harvard Graphics and others)

Table 4.1: Standard Document Exchange Formats (cont'd)

Function	Format
Graphic (cont.)	
	DXF (AutoCad)
	CDR (Corel Draw)
	WPG (WordPerfect Graphics)
Spreadsheets	
	1-2-3 (.WK3, WK1, and .WKS file extensions)
	Excel (.XLS file extension)
	SYLK (Symbolic Link Format)
	DIF (Data Interchange Format)
	DBF (Database File)
	CSV (Common Separated Values)
Database	
	dBASE II, III, and IV (.DBF file extension)

Some applications support file formats outside their own functional groups. For example, since both spreadsheets and databases read and write data in tabular format, some spreadsheet applications can read database files, and vice versa.

If you use one of these formats to exchange files and you do not get proper results, experiment with the other formats—each tends to produce slightly different results.

FILE SHARING TIP #2: Get a Few Widely Used Applications

If your business depends on being able to share files with other computer users while on the road, it is wise to purchase a set of the "standard" applications. Our recommendations are as follows:

- WordPerfect or Microsoft Word for word processing
- Lotus 1-2-3 or Microsoft Excel for spreadsheets
- dBASE, Paradox, or FoxPro for databases
- PageMaker or Ventura Publisher for document layout
- Corel Draw or Micrographix Designer for graphics

Armed with just a few of these applications, you'll have many more options available than are provided with some of the lesser-known products. Although these products are by no means inexpensive, you must carefully weigh their cost against the problems that you may encounter without them. If you do not want to buy these particular applications, make sure that the applications you purchase have full file compatibility with the majority of them.

If you cannot use applications that include format-conversion capabilities, you should purchase a file-conversion utility. Chapters 5 and 7 provide more information about file-transfer utility packages.

Transferring Font Information

Even when you have successfully exchanged a file between applications, its fonts might not have come with it. This is usually the case when the importing and exporting applications reside on different systems and attach to different printers. Since DOS provides no centralized font management facility (as Windows does), the fonts specified in a document are tied almost exclusively to native printer fonts, printer font cartridges, and downloadable (*soft*) fonts.

Exchanging Files on the Road   **47**

For example, if you are importing a WordPerfect 5.0 document that has various fonts specified at different locations in the text, there is no guarantee that this information can be communicated effectively to another application on a different system. The system on which this file is being imported may not have the correct soft font, native printer font, or printer font cartridge to replicate the original fonts within the document. In this case, the font may be disregarded or a *font substitution* may take place, where the importing application uses the available font which most resembles the original one.

Font problems can arise even when you are using Windows, which provides a font management facility. For example, suppose a Windows application document created on one system has New Century Schoolbook, Palatino, and Optima specified as its three main fonts. If you bring this document into a different system that does not have these fonts installed, other fonts will be substituted for the original fonts, and you may not be pleased with the results.

See Chapter 6 for more information about font support.

FIVE

Using Utility Packages to Avoid Disaster

Utility packages are essential for successful computing with a desktop machine, but they are even more critical for survival with a laptop machine. There are a number of utilities that can at one time or another save your life. Many of these utilities will be useful for everyday computing, while others will be called to active duty on rare occasions. In the end, using any of these utilities should save you time and energy and protect the investment you have made in a laptop computer.

DOS Can Provide Some Utility Answers

MS-DOS provides more than just the operating system platform on which laptop computers work. Depending on the version you are using, MS-DOS includes many utilities that provide solid benefits to a laptop user. For example, the most widely distributed version (3.31) provides more than 80 commands that can help users work with their systems more effectively. Newer versions of MS-DOS have even more features, such as a graphical user interface (or shell) and the ability to manage RAM more effectively.

Some of the MS-DOS utility functions and the commands used to run them are as follows:

- Configure a new disk (FORMAT)
- Back up your data (BACKUP)
- Copy files (COPY)
- Delete files (DEL)
- Create batch processes (COPYCON)
- Edit a text file (EDLIN)
- View a list of files (DIR)

See Chapter 13 for a guide to MS-DOS commands.

Using Utility Packages to Avoid Disaster

DOS UTILITY TIP #1: Upgrade to MS-DOS 5.0

Is MS-DOS 5.0 worth the cost of upgrading? This version has many new features, and among them are utilities previously provided by only the better third-party software companies. To buy the equivalent benefits of MS-DOS 5.0 without purchasing DOS 5.0 would require the following:

- PC Tools version 7.0 (about $120 retail) for the disk utilities and full-screen text editor
- QEMM 386 (about $60 retail) for the memory management
- A DOS command utility program (about $40) for the functions of the DOSKEY command

The total cost is over $200, versus MS-DOS 5.0's retail price of about $75. We recommend upgrading to MS-DOS 5.0 simply for the four major new utilities that come with it:

- Mirror: This utility will back up your file allocation table (FAT), which is the bookkeeper of your system. If this table on your laptop computer's hard disk is corrupted, your files and programs are not necessarily destroyed, but the file that kept track of their location is gone. This feature makes a copy (mirror) of that table, so that a file (using Undelete) or an entire hard disk (using Rebuild) can be restored properly.

- Undelete: This utility can restore a file that has been deleted with the MS-DOS DEL command.

- Rebuild: This utility will restore a disk erased by the MS-DOS FORMAT command or any file in the root directory erased by the MS-DOS DEL command. It can also rebuild a corrupted disk partition table. Rebuild works best if the Mirror utility has been used recently, but it can also rebuild the disk without the use of the mirrored file, in a slower and less reliable fashion.

- DOSKEY: This terminate-and-stay-resident (TSR) utility allows you to customize and automate MS-DOS command lines. (A TSR utility is a program that loads into memory and is available for use even while other applications are running.)

The Jack of All Trades

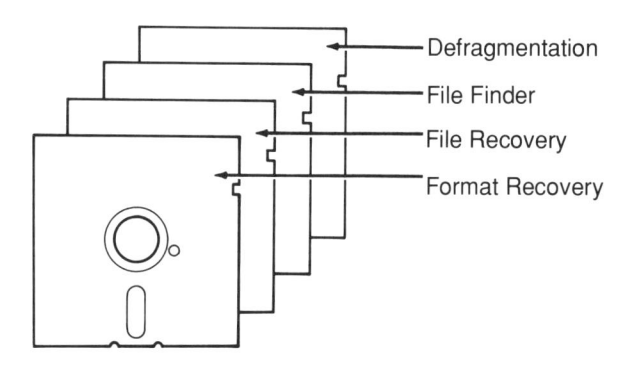

- Defragmentation
- File Finder
- File Recovery
- Format Recovery

The primary goal of MS-DOS is to be a general operating system. Its implementation of utilities is secondary in importance to overall system stability and functionality. Another reason the utilities in MS-DOS are somewhat lacking is that they must support the lowest common denominator in machine types and adhere to the most rigid of standards. MS-DOS's lack of a robust set of utilities has paved the way for a whole market of products that can help laptop users.

The best packages are the standard DOS toolkits, such as Mace Utilities, The Norton Utilities, or PC Tools.

A standard DOS package will suit most laptop users because it includes a variety of utilities that perform their functions acceptably. If you are wondering why you should buy one of these utilities, the following reasons alone will justify the cost.

Using Utility Packages to Avoid Disaster

TOOLKIT TIP #1: Have a Format Disaster Plan

Whether you are in your office or on the road, if you lose the *formatting* of your hard disk and do not have a backup copy of your data, you will need to use a utility to recover from the disaster.

Mace Utilities, The Norton Utilities, and PC Tools Deluxe all offer a hard-disk format recovery function. You may never need to use such a utility, but having it on hand provides you with a disaster recovery plan.

TOOLKIT TIP #2: Avoid the DEL *.* Blues

The ability to recover a file that had been accidentally deleted was the main feature of all early DOS utility programs. For example, PC Tools provides a utility called Undelete to perform this function. The importance of this feature has not diminished over time.

Without a file-recovery utility or backup copy of the deleted file, you have no way to restore the file. Even if you have a recent backup copy, you will lose the information entered since you made that copy. Having this utility on hand makes file recovery quick and painless.

TOOLKIT TIP #3: Find the Needle in the Haystack

Laptop owners usually spend a great deal more time exchanging files between their machine and another machine than desktop computer users. Although the problems involved in the exchange of files may be obvious, there is a related problem that is not. This constant trading of files can sometimes make the management of file names, locations, and versions a challenging endeavor.

Having a file- and text-finding utility can save you a great deal of time and effort in accessing your data. All of the standard DOS toolkits include a function to locate files and text on your disk.

And the Winner Is . . .

So which utility toolkit should you get? We have found that PC Tools (version 6.0 or 7.0) is the best of the general utilities group, with The Norton Utilities and Mace Utilities close behind.

PC Tools provides command-line shortcuts and excellent use of the mouse. You can easily launch any of its well-designed utilities.

Hard-Disk-Management Utilities Revisited

In Chapter 3, we discussed the use of defragmentation and compression utilities to manage your hard disk. All the DOS toolkit packages we have mentioned in this chapter include a disk defragmentation utility to reorganize the locations of files on your hard disk into a logical order. Along with improving file handling, using such a utility can speed up the recovery of files that were accidentally deleted.

Another utility recommended in Chapter 3 is PKZIP, which compresses and archives files. If you do not need regular access to a file, use a compression or archiving program to compress it. Programs such as PKZIP or LHARC compress a file by replacing repeated information with short strings of characters that take up less room. When you need access to the file, it can be decompressed.

Compression and archiving programs are also useful for getting a group of files compressed into one file so that they can be copied to a floppy disk for transfer to another machine or for backup purposes. Another good reason for grouping files into one archived file is that this reduces the 4K of overhead DOS unilaterally requires for every file.

How much wasted space is in your files? Below is a sample of space reductions using PKZIP 1.1 with popular software program file formats:

- Word processors

    Microsoft Word: 52%

    WordPerfect: 52%

Using Utility Packages to Avoid Disaster

Multimate Advantage: 64%
Word for Windows: 52%
WordStar: 63%

- Spreadsheets and database formats

Microsoft Excel: 57%
VisiCalc: 65%
Lotus 1-2-3: 62%
Data Interchange Format: 81%
dBASE: 78%

Getting Files to and from Your Laptop Faster

It is likely that there will be times when it is critical for you to move a whole directory of files from your laptop computer to another computer nearby. With similar floppy disk drives or an archiving utility, you can physically transfer the files, but these solutions lack a feature that may be crucial for success: speed.

FILE MOVEMENT TIP #1: Use a Transfer Utility

As mentioned in Chapter 1, if you need to move large amounts of data on a regular basis, save yourself some time and eliminate potential frustration by purchasing a file-transfer program. The file-transfer utility market is relatively mature and offers a number of extremely good alternatives for the laptop computer owner.

The Brooklyn Bridge, LapLink III, WinConnect, and Fast Lynx are programs that provide file-transfer capabilities. All of these are good programs; our favorite is LapLink III, which we have used with great success. See Chapter 7 for more information about transferring files with a utility.

Keeping Your Files Clean

Like it or not, there are some individuals who think writing a program to cause a computer some problems is an accomplishment. This has changed the connotation of the title *computer hacker* from positive to negative. A computer *virus* is a program that is able to distribute itself from one system to another by a variety of means that are undetected by the user. Viruses can have a number of effects. Some are *benign,* meaning that they cause no real harm, while others can delete some or all of your data and cripple your system.

CLEANSING UTILITY TIP #1: Protect Your Files from Viruses

Because it travels more than a desktop computer, a laptop computer is going to perform many file transfers with outside sources. To avoid problems, you should purchase a virus-protection software package.

We do not enjoy having to write on this subject or even having to include it as part of our book, but we have seen the results of data loss and system-security violation caused by computer virus programs. It is not a laughing matter. In some cases, it has cost people their jobs, even though they did not write or deliberately load the infected program. Scan and Cleanup are two of the most widely recognized virus programs on the market.

Reading the File Once You Get It

We have talked about locating files, keeping their integrity, and even transferring them from machine to machine. But what if the document you are about to transfer or receive is in a format that will be foreign or unacceptable to the software package that ultimately needs to use it?

READING TIP #1: Get a File-Conversion Utility

In Chapter 4, we discussed the problem of sharing files that are from different programs. We recommended that you use programs that have adequate format-conversion capabilities. If your software does not offer enough formats in which to save your files, you can purchase a utility that can convert from or to many of the different program file formats.

The advantage of a file-conversion utility is that you can keep intact not only the content of your work but also the formatting characteristics of your document. This will save hours of unnecessary rekeying and reformatting of work already performed.

If your applications are lacking in format-conversion capabilities, we recommend that you purchase a file-conversion utility such as Software Bridge.

SIX

Printing on the Road

At your home or office, printing is rarely an issue. The appropriate printer drivers are already loaded on your system, the right fonts are available to your applications, and your computer is properly connected to your printer.

On the road, however, the situation can be quite different because it may be necessary to print your documents on printers that you have not used before. There are a number of things that can go wrong, and you won't necessarily have the time or knowledge to solve problems. In this chapter, the potential obstacles to printing on the road are discussed, along with tips and solutions for avoiding them.

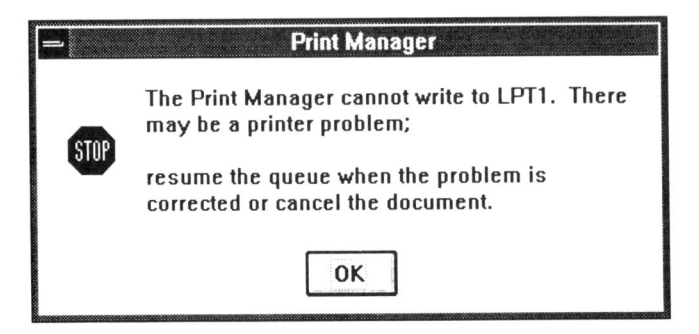

Avoiding Show Stoppers

> **Print Manager**
>
> The Print Manager cannot write to LPT1. There may be a printer problem;
>
> resume the queue when the problem is corrected or cancel the document.
>
> OK

When you are printing a document to an unknown printer, a variety of problems can arise. Some of these problems fall into the category of "annoyances" that prevent you from getting your output exactly how you want, and some problems fall into the category of "show stoppers," which prevent you from printing at all. The following are the most common obstacles to printing on the road:

- You do not have the right cable to communicate with the printer.
- You do not have the right length of cable to reach the printer.

Printing on the Road 61

- You do not have the right interface on your laptop to communicate with the printer.
- You do not have the right printer driver on your system.
- The printer lacks sufficient memory to print your document.

With a small amount of preparation, most of these show stoppers are preventable, and you'll be able to print your documents no matter where you go. Before you leave home base with your laptop, make sure to consider the following tips.

PRINTING TIP #1: Battle Gear Tip #7 Revisited

As we suggested in Chapter 1, one way to avoid printing problems is to bring your own printer cable. To make sure that you can connect your laptop to the printer, bring a 10- to 15-foot long cable. If you are not sure which type of printer will be available, take both a serial and parallel connector cable. Figure 6.1 shows the difference between a parallel and serial cable interface.

9-Pin Serial Interface   25-Pin Parallel Interface

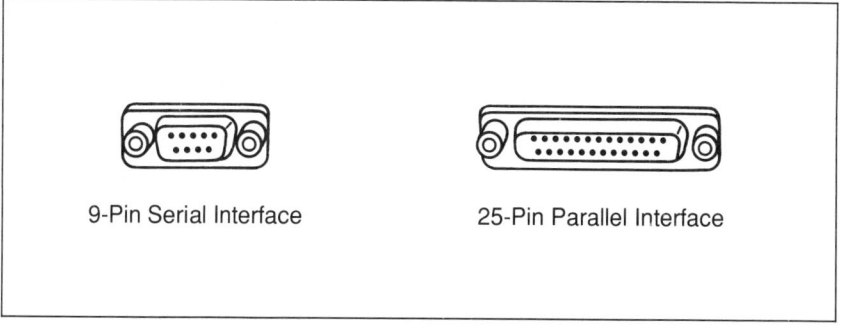

Figure 6.1: Parallel and serial interfaces

Another option is to take a parallel-serial converter with you, as described in the next tip.

PRINTING TIP #2: Take an Interface Converter

Many laptops have both a serial and a parallel port, but some come without a parallel interface. In most cases, the parallel port is used for the printer, and the serial port can be used for either a printer or modem. Whatever your configuration, there is always the possibility that your laptop's interface will not be compatible with the printer's interface.

One way to avoid the incompatability issue is to carry a small serial-to-parallel or parallel-to-serial converter, which takes data in one format and converts it to the other.

PRINTING TIP #3: Take a Variety of Printer Drivers

When you select the Print option within an application such as Word, PageMaker, or Lotus 1-2-3, your application sends the document to a printer driver. A *printer driver* is a software package that converts the application's native data format into a series of commands that the printer can understand.

Since there are different command sets as well as different versions of the same command set, you need to use the printer driver that sends the printer the right commands. MS-DOS applications, without Windows, come with a variety of their own printer drivers. The Windows environment provides a set of universal drivers that all applications can use, so you do not need different drivers for each application.

Regardless of your laptop's environment (MS-DOS or Windows), you should take a good selection of printer drivers with you on the road. There are several ways to bring them.

If you have Windows, you can take copies of your Windows master disks. The printer drivers are located on one of these disks, and you can load the one you need by running the Windows Control Panel program, or by selecting the Printer Setup option on the File menu of most Windows applications. When you choose Printers from the Control Panel, you will see a dialog box similar to the one shown in Figure 6.2.

Printing on the Road 63

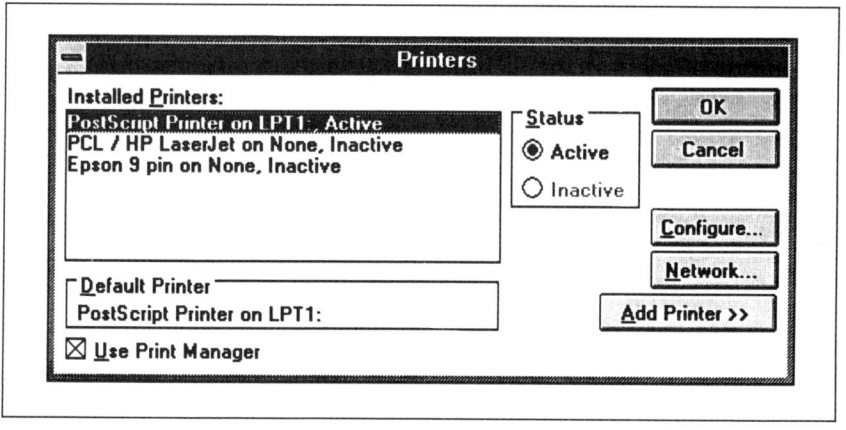

Figure 6.2: Using the Windows Control Panel to change printer drivers

If you do not have Windows, you can take the appropriate master disk copies of all the applications that you plan to print with on the road.

An alternative to taking copies of master disks is to bring a copy of just the disk containing the printer drivers, or copy the appropriate drivers to your hard disk. For example, to create a printer definition in WordPerfect 5.1, follow these steps:

1. Press Shift-F7 to choose to print.
2. Type S to select a printer.
3. Type A to choose additional printers.
4. Place the cursor on the desired printer and press Enter to select it.
5. If it cannot find the driver on your hard disk, WordPerfect will prompt you to insert the disk containing the appropriate printer driver. Insert the disk and press Enter to continue.
6. Press Enter to accept WordPerfect's name for the printer.
7. Press F7 to exit.

Another way to bring a variety of printer drivers with you is to preinstall the drivers you are likely to need. If you do not know which types of printers you will use, preinstall the most common ones:

- PostScript
- HPPCL
- Epson (9-pin or 24-pin)
- IBM Proprinter

These four drivers are compatible with most of the printers currently in use.

PRINTING TIP #4: Confirm that You'll Have Enough Printer Memory

Generally speaking, there are four basic types of printers: daisy-wheel, dot-matrix, laser, and ink-jet. Of these four types, the laser is the only one that comes with a significant amount of memory. This is because laser printers are actually specialized computers, complete with a CPU, RAM, and ROM (read-only memory). When printer instructions representing a document are downloaded to a laser printer, the CPU inside the printer converts the instructions to a series of dots (a *bit-map*) on a page. These printer instructions are stored in the printer's own RAM.

In some cases, documents, especially those with graphics, can exceed the RAM capacity of the laser printer. The only recourse is to divide the document into smaller files and print each one individually or add new printer RAM. Daisy-wheel and dot-matrix printers do not process a series of instructions, and thus do not need local RAM.

If you are creating memos, letters, and other documents that consist mostly of text without graphics, most laser printers should have enough memory to print your documents. However, if you are running graphics-oriented applications such as PageMaker, Ventura Publisher, or Corel Draw, your documents will not print properly on a printer with a small amount of RAM.

Printing on the Road

If possible, before you travel, call ahead to where you will be printing documents to confirm that enough printer RAM is available. If not, try to coordinate the addition of some memory to the printer. You can use the following guidelines for minimum requirements:

Word processing, no graphics	512K
Word processing, with graphics	1MB
Drawing and illustration software	2MB
Small to medium spreadsheets	512K
Large spreadsheets	1MB
Page layout	2MB

What You Get Is Not What You Want

Suppose your laptop computer is finally connected to a printer that your software and printer driver will support, but the printed document looks nothing like you thought it would. If you are a veteran laptop user, this probably is a familiar predicament when printing on the road.

Printing tips #1 through #5 will help to ensure that your laptop computer will properly connect to a unfamiliar printer. They will not, however, guarantee that the printed document will look the same as when you printed it at home or in your office.

WYSIWYG TIP #1: Make Sure
Your Application Can Control Page Setup

An important function of your software application and its related printer driver is to send the proper page-dimension commands to the printer. With most of today's software packages, you can simply select the Page Setup option from a menu, and then modify the specifications so that they conform to what you will be printing and the capabilities of the printer you will be using. See Chapter 13 for specific page-setup commands for several software applications.

Most laser printers can print to within ¼ inch of the edges of the paper. On an 8½-inch by 11-inch page, most dot-matrix and daisy-wheel printers will print 80 characters across.

WYSIWYG TIP #2: Use Soft Fonts for Font Support

Font support is a subject that needs a separate book to be covered properly. The issue of font support is complicated because there is no single industry standard guiding how fonts are defined, stored, or used. Users are penalized because each application or printer works with fonts in a different manner.

Fonts are separated into two categories: bit-map and outline. *Bit-maps* are pixels that form each character. The typeface bit-maps reside either on your laptop's hard disk or in the printer's memory. An individual bit-map is required for each single character representing a single point size and type style. For example, the letter Z in 8-point Helvetica must use one bit-map, while the same letter in 10-point Helvetica must use a different bit-map. The ability to use bold and italic versions of the letter requires even more bit-maps. To put things in perspective, a single ASCII character set needs about 100 bit-maps per point size. The use of a variety of typefaces can push the storage capacity of your laptop's hard disk to its limit.

Bit-map fonts create another problem as well: the need for two different sets of fonts. One bit-map is needed for your screen and another for your printer. This is because the monitor's resolution is about 70 to 80 dots per inch (dpi), and printers can print from 70 to 300 dpi. Bit-map characters are resolution-dependent, which means that a 10-point Helvetica bit-map may look fine on your screen but be virtually unreadable on a 300-dpi laser printer.

When a screen font is installed, it remains on your disk until you need it for use in an application. Each one can either be loaded into RAM before you run your application or selected after you start your application.

Printer fonts are handled differently. They are either resident within a printer's ROM, installed through ROM font cartridges, or downloaded to the printer from the computer (soft fonts). Soft fonts may be downloaded prior to or at print time, depending on the application. Soft fonts must be downloaded to the printer each time it is turned on or reset.

A newer approach is to supply fonts as outlines. *Outline* fonts (sometimes called *scalable* fonts) are mathematical descriptions of characters from which printer or screen bit-map fonts are built when needed. The mathematical formulas are actually Bezier curves that sketch the outside edges of each character. The advantage of outline fonts is that you can build multiple point sizes and type styles from a single outline representation. This saves disk space and makes font configuration much simpler. Outlines also let you build both printer fonts and screen fonts from a single mathematical description.

Soft fonts are created with either a type manager (a combination font generator, installer, and manager), such as Facelift from Bitstream or Type Manager from Adobe, or you can buy already prepared printer soft fonts, such as the Adobe Type Library from Adobe Systems. Although both of these types are technically soft fonts, they work in a different fashion. Printer soft fonts are downloaded to the printer from your computer and incorporated into your document by the printer. Type managers create fonts in the computer and incorporate them into the document before sending it to the printer.

Printer soft fonts generally have smoother edges and more consistency. One printer soft font may cost $10 to $15, while a package of outline fonts may cost around $195. However, a complete package of printer soft fonts costs as much or more than a package of outline fonts that will be used by a type manager. A type manager also has the advantage of not requiring extra hard-disk space to store each bit-map image, as printer soft fonts do.

If you need only a few typefaces and are using one specific printer, we recommend that you use printer soft fonts because of their overall quality and price. If you are using MS-DOS applications, printer soft fonts are actually your only reasonable solution because type managers do not work outside the Windows environment.

To make use of a printer soft font, you must configure each MS-DOS application to acknowledge the font. Although this is time-consuming when you use a wide variety of MS-DOS applications that support soft fonts, it is a much better solution than using printer font cartridges (see WYSIWYG Tip #3). Consult your MS-DOS application manuals for more information about font support.

If you have Windows, need a wider variety of typefaces, use different printers, and do not have the hard-disk space to store all the required bit-maps, using a type manager is a better idea. With Windows applications, the issue of font support is less complicated because Windows makes every installed font available to all applications. For example, using Adobe Type Manager and its standard 13 fonts allows any Windows application to use all 13 of the fonts shown in Figure 6.3. An additional benefit is that all 13 fonts can be output to any printer that has a Windows driver.

WYSIWYG TIP #3: Forget About Printer Cartridges

Printer font cartridges were the original way to add more fonts to a printer. They are usually plugged into a slot located at the base of the printer and add about four typefaces per cartridge. Font cartridges are not appropriate for laptop computing because different printers use different font cartridges and carrying them around adds extra baggage. The same can be said about PostScript cartridges. Type managers eliminate the need to use printer-specific hardware.

Printing on the Road 69

```
Courier
Courier Bold
Courier Bold Italic
Courier Italic
```

Helvetica
Helvetica Bold
Helvetica Bold Italic
Helvetica Italic

```
Symbol
```

Times
Times Bold
Times Bold Italic
Times Italic

Figure 6.3: The standard 13 fonts available with Adobe Type Manager

SEVEN

Laptop-to-Desktop File Transfer

There will undoubtedly be times when you must transfer files from your laptop to another computer. In many cases, two floppy disk drives (one on each machine) and a diskette are all you need to successfully transfer data back and forth. But often a good file-transfer utility is much better suited for the job, especially with large numbers of files.

Transferring Large Amounts of Data

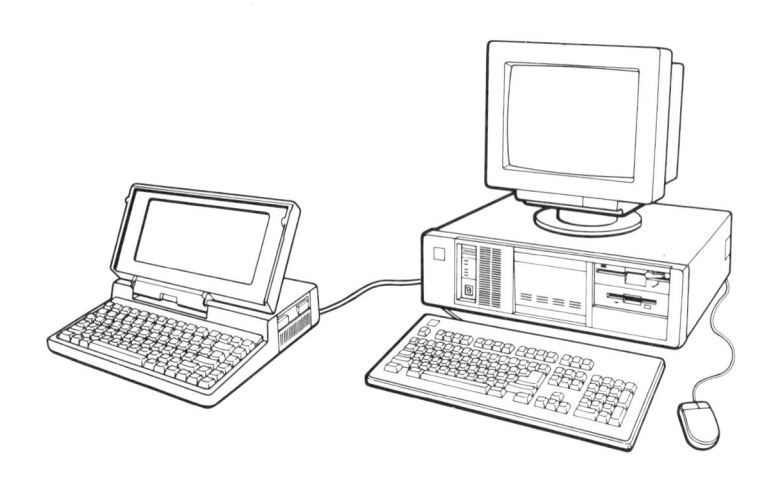

File-transfer utilities work by setting up a communications channel between the serial or parallel ports on both computers. A cable (usually provided by the utility manufacturer) is attached to one port on each computer (either the serial port on both or the parallel port on both), the software is started on both machines, and you can then control the transfer of data in either direction.

Laptop-to-Desktop File Transfer

HEFTY TRANSFER TIP #1: Use a Utility Instead of a Disk Drive

If you plan on transferring large amounts of data frequently, we recommend that you purchase a file-transfer utility, such as Traveling Software's LapLink or Fifth Generation Systems' The Brooklyn Bridge. These utilities are relatively inexpensive and offer the following advantages over standard floppy disk drive transfer:

- The data transfer rate is faster than with a floppy disk drive— about 250K per second with a serial connection and 500K per second with a parallel connection. Even with a 1.44MB floppy disk drive, you must still copy files onto a floppy disk, insert the disk into the other computer, and copy the files again. This multiple-step process takes much longer.

- You can perform selective file transfers, which means that you can transfer certain files in the directory tree and not transfer others. You can also select all subdirectories in a particular directory for transfer with one step. (The MS-DOS XCOPY command copies directory structures but does not allow exclusion of individual files.)

- With a file-transfer utility, you never need to worry about floppy disk drive compatibility problems. If one computer has a 3½-inch 720K drive and the other computer has only a 5¼-inch 1.2MB drive, as long as both of them have a serial port (virtually all do), you can transfer files without a problem.

HEFTY TRANSFER TIP #2: Maintain Mirrored Directories

File-transfer utilities are especially useful if you have a laptop and a desktop on which you want to maintain mirrored directories. *Mirroring* data between your laptop and desktop means that you periodically update each computer's hard disk to keep identical sets of files (directories) on both machines.

The mirrored directory approach, although requiring a bit more effort, ensures that you always have a reasonably recent backup copy of all your files, including data files and applications. The only files that remain different are system files, such as AUTOEXEC.BAT, CONFIG.SYS, and WIN.INI. This replication of data on two systems makes owning a laptop a safer proposition.

Using LapLink on the Road

Using LapLink is fairly straightforward. If you have the LapLink program installed on your laptop (usually in the LL3 directory at the root level) and you want to connect to another computer that doesn't have LapLink (which we'll call the *target* computer) follow these steps:

1. Attach your LapLink cables to the appropriate ports on each computer. Use the parallel port on both devices if possible, because data transfer will be much faster than with a serial connection. If the parallel port is not available on one of the computers, use the serial port connectors (either 9-pin or 25-pin). Do **not** connect the cable to a serial port on one device and a parallel port on the other because this might damage both computers.

2. If the target computer does not have LapLink, you need to install the program on its hard disk. First, create a subdirectory named LL3 on the target computer at the root level by typing the command **MD \LL3** and pressing Enter.

3. Change to the LL3 directory on the target computer by typing **CD \LL3** and pressing Enter.

4. Insert a floppy disk that contains the file LAPLINK.EXE into the target computer, type **COPY A:LL3.EXE,** and press Enter. This installs a copy of the LapLink program onto the target computer's hard disk.

5. From within the LL3 directory on both machines, type **LL3** and press Enter to start LapLink.

Laptop-to-Desktop File Transfer 75

You should now see the LapLink screen, shown in Figure 7.1, on both computers.

```
                              DOS Window
LapLink (3.00)  Copyright 1986-89  Traveling Software Inc.  06-28-91   1:50pm
=== Local Drive (C:) 16793600 Free
         <PARENT DIR> 04-01-91   1:32p        <PARENT DIR> 04-01-91   1:32p
         <ROOT   DIR> 04-01-91   1:32p        <ROOT   DIR> 04-01-91   1:32p
LL3      .EXE   93399 06-05-91   7:09a   LL3  .EXE   93399 06-05-91   7:09a
B&B      .PM3  262144 03-27-91   2:35p   B&B  .PM3  262144 03-27-91   2:35p
DOS5JHL  .PM3  104704 03-09-91  11:24a   DOS5JHL .PM3 104704 03-09-91 11:24a
USWEST   .PM3  164096 02-12-91   2:45p   USWEST .PM3 164096 02-12-91   2:45p
42       .PM3  145664 01-16-91  10:57p   42   .PM3  145664 01-16-91  10:57p
37       .PM3  114176 01-16-91  10:41p   37   .PM3  114176 01-16-91  10:41p
25       .PM3  171136 01-16-91  10:03p   25   .PM3  171136 01-16-91  10:03p
20       .PM3  158080 01-16-91   9:06p   20   .PM3  158080 01-16-91   9:06p
15       .PM3  171264 01-16-91   8:12p   15   .PM3  171264 01-16-91   8:12p




= C:\LAPLINK
                                              SN HR    T  COM2:   9600
    Help Log Find Wildcopy Copy Erase Tag GroupTag UngroupTag AgainTag Quit More→

        Accessories   US West   Perkins Coie  Games  SQLWindows  Main
```

Figure 7.1: LapLink opening screen

If you see a message indicating that the systems cannot connect with each other, press **O** to display the Option screen. Select the Transfer Mode option and then select Parallel or Serial, depending on which cable connector you have used. Also, make sure you have specified the correct ports through which you will send data. For parallel communications, this will be either LPT1 or LPT on both devices. For serial communications, this will usually be either COM1 or COM2 on both devices.

EIGHT

Effective Remote Communications

Most of us bought laptops because we needed to work while away from the office. In buying this ability to work on the road, we created the need to communicate with other devices, such as remote computers or fax machines, at any given time. Along with your off-site communication requirements, your laptop might have to handle network connections upon return to the office. You may find that there are not enough slots in your laptop to have all these capabilities.

This chapter focuses on the optimum laptop configuration and modem setup for effective remote communication. Chapter 9 covers networking requirements, and Chapter 10 provides suggestions for giving your laptop faxing capabilities.

Configuring Your Laptop for Remote Communication

Is there any way to have powerful remote communication and acceptable network connection capabilities in the same laptop computer? The answer is yes. In fact, your biggest problem may be sorting out all the available solutions.

If you are using a laptop that has a couple of standard slots or an expansion chassis, the issue of outside communications and network connectivity is not overly complicated. For the most part, the solution will involve using the same modems, fax boards, and network cards for your laptop that are being used by your (or your company's) desktop computer. If, however, you are running out of slots, purchase a fax-modem board (as recommended in Chapter 1) from the same manufacturer of the desktop computer's modem.

REMOTE CONNECTIVITY TIP #1:
Uniformity Can Be an Advantage

If you have a laptop computer with at least two standard AT slots, you should purchase devices that are the same make and model as those used in your office. This approach will ensure that the laptop system will work with the computer at the home office. Having common components can also reduce the complexity of telephone support while on the road, because both the support person and the user are working with the same device.

REMOTE CONNECTIVITY TIP #2:
Avoid Using an Expansion Chassis

If you have a laptop with at least two standard slots, we suggest that you avoid using an expansion chassis unless you really need the extra slots. Some expansion chassis do not provide reliable connections and may fail during remote communication. If you must purchase one, get some advice from the manufacturer of your laptop before making the investment. See Chapter 9 for more information about expansion chassis.

Your Slot Options

If you're using a laptop that has one or no standard slots (for example, a notebook computer), you must deal with the problem of limited expansion room, which makes remote communications more complicated. Some manufacturers provide only proprietary slots, which will not work with industry-standard cards, in their laptops. To use these proprietary slots, you must purchase devices made specifically for your computer, usually from the laptop manufacturer. More often than not, this means your choices are limited. The most common device available for the proprietary slot is a modem or fax modem.

If you have a laptop computer that has one or no standard slots, use the proprietary slot for a modem or, as recommended in Chapter 2, a fax modem. The standard slot can be used for the network card. If there is no standard slot available, you can use an external network connection device that attaches to your laptop's parallel port (see Chapters 1 and 9 for a discussion on network adapters).

Here are our suggestions for laptop configurations:

- A laptop with two standard slots and one proprietary slot:
  - Slot 1: extra serial port (if needed)
  - Slot 2: network card (if needed)
  - Proprietary: fax modem or modem
- A laptop with one standard slot and one proprietary slot:
  - Slot 1: extra serial port (if needed)
  - Proprietary: fax modem or modem
- A laptop with no standard slot and one proprietary slot:
  - Proprietary: fax modem or modem
  - Parallel printer port: pocket LAN adapter (if needed)
- A laptop with no slots:
  - Serial port: fax modem or modem
  - Parallel printer port: pocket LAN adapter (if needed)

The Importance of How Your Modem Operates

Effective Remote Communications

If you have already purchased and installed a modem, the information presented here can help you set it up for optimal performance. If you do not have a modem yet, read this and the following sections to get an idea of which modem features are important for working with a laptop computer.

MODEM TIP #1: Use an Internal Modem

As a laptop user, you should use an internal modem versus a standard (not pocket) external modem because of what it doesn't require:

- No additional power supply
- No reliance on wall plug outlets
- No extra cables to connect
- No extra desktop space
- No need to disable existing serial port connections

Most internal modems can be assigned to operate on the serial port COM1, COM2, COM3, or COM4, as illustrated in Figure 8.1. A modem with this capability will be useful if your laptop already has COM1 and COM2 built in. This way, you can avoid having to disable an existing COM port in order for your modem to work. Another option with its own set of benefits is a pocket fax modem (see Chapters 1 and 10 for more information).

MODEM TIP #2: Make Your Modem Work Properly with Windows

When you use a modem while running Windows, a problem can arise if you try to take advantage of multiple serial connections (such as a mouse and modem) that are not in sequential order. For example, if you have

Port	Switch	Address	IRQ
COM1	↓⧫⧫⧫☐ ON 1 2 3 4	3F8H	4
COM2	↓☐⧫⧫☐ ON 1 2 3 4	2F8H	3
COM3	↓⧫☐⧫☐ ON 1 2 3 4	3E8H	4
COM4	↓☐☐☐☐ ON 1 2 3 4	2E8H	3

Figure 8.1: Intel 2400-bps internal modem switch settings

your laptop set up so that the mouse is connected to COM1, no device is connected to COM2, and a modem is connected to COM3, the modem will not transmit data properly.

Windows requires that serial ports be used in logical order and that any mouse connection be to COM1 or COM2. If you have a laptop with two existing serial ports (COM1 and COM2) and an internal modem, and you plan on using Windows, here is our suggested configuration (the actual settings depend on the laptop you are using):

- Connect your mouse to the existing COM1 port.

- Reconfigure your laptop's existing COM2 port as COM3. If you cannot reconfigure this port, you will have to disable it altogether.

- Configure your internal modem as COM2.

Figure 8.2 illustrates this configuration.

Effective Remote Communications   83

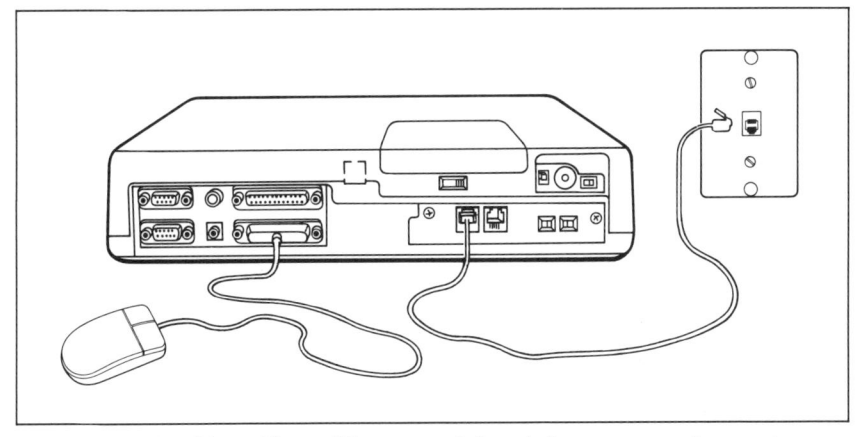

Figure 8.2: Avoid conflicts with your serial ports by proper assignments

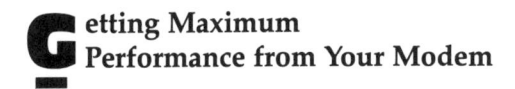

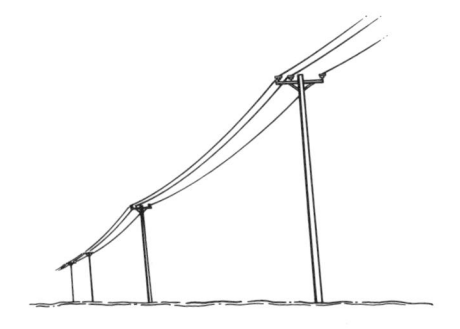

Getting Maximum Performance from Your Modem

There are three factors that govern a modem's performance:

- Transfer speed
- Error control
- Data compression

Telephone lines are typically not very cooperative in moving data with quickness and reliability. The telephone line was designed to transmit voice analog signals, not the digital electronic signals generated by computers. Modems convert the electronic signals generated by the computer into tones the telephone line will accept. The bandwidth of the telephone line, however, limits how fast these audio tones can change frequency in order to represent computer data (zeros and ones).

Modem transfer rates stayed in the 300 to 1200 bits per second (bps) range because of the lack of an inexpensive modem chip set and the lack of compatibility due to varying modulation standards. In the United States, Bell 103 and 212A were the accepted modulation schemes. Virtually every other country adhered to the Comité Consultatif Internationale Telegraphique et Telephonic (CCITT) V.21 and V.22 standards.

In the 1980s, modem manufacturers started making a modem chip that uses the 2400-bps protocol established by CCITT V.22 standards while maintaining compatibility with the Bell and CCITT 300-bps and 1200-bps protocols.

MODEM TIP #3: Purchase a Powerful Modem

Because compatability is not a problem for modems meeting the V.22 standard, we do not recommend purchasing a new modem with anything less than a 2400-bps transfer rate. This transfer rate will be sufficient for most users of bulletin boards or other on-line systems. A 2400-bps modem costs between $100 and $150.

If, however, you are going to transfer large amounts of data, we suggest using a 4800-bps or 9600-bps modem. A 4800-bps modem costs between $250 and $400, and a 9600-bps modem is priced between $475 and $700. But don't buy a higher speed modem unless you know that you will be exchanging data with modems that have corresponding transfer rates.

MODEM TIP #4: Get a Modem with Built-in Error Control

If you need to improve your modem's transfer speed to above 2400 bps, you must improve transfer accuracy as well. This is because of the telephone line limitations mentioned earlier. Greater accuracy can be achieved through error-control techniques used by the modem hardware.

Modems that incorporate the Microcom Network Protocols (MNP) 2 through 4 or the CCITT V.42 protocol take advantage of the current standards for error control. These newer techniques also work independently of modulation schemes. Therefore, 4800-bps and 9600-bps modems can offer the same error-control schemes. The V.42 error control does provide an advantage in that it incorporates the Linked Access Packet (LAP)-M error-control protocol as its primary method of correction and MNP 2 through 4 as its alternative method.

Both the MNP and V.42 protocols funnel the data being transmitted into segments, or packets, of information. Included with each packet is a *cyclical redundancy check* (CRC), 16-bit for MNP and 16- or 32-bit for V.42. The CRC analyzes the content of the packet in statistical form. The receiving modem independently conducts the same analysis as the packet comes in. If the CRCs do not match properly, the receiving modem will request that the packet be sent again. For any of these methods to work, the modems on both sides of the line must support the same protocols and compression standards.

You can increase your data-transfer speed and reliability by utilizing the error-control capabilities offered by the MNP or V.42 protocols. When data is sent with no error-correction requirements, it takes 10 bits to transmit a single byte: one start bit, eight data bits, and one stop bit. This means your 2400-bps modem, working without any hardware or software enhancements, can send only at 240 bytes per second, and without error-control protection.

Not only can modems with the MNP or V.42 protocols provide error-control protection during the entire transmittal session, they also can actually improve throughput (about 20 to 25 percent, to 275 bps) as well. If you are going to purchase a modem with V.42 capabilities, make sure that it is V.42 *compliant*, not just V.42 *compatible*. A modem that is V.42

compliant will use LAP-M as its primary error-control protocol and MNP 2 through 4 as the alternative protocol. A modem that is V.42 compatible may offer only MNP 2 through 4 error control.

MODEM TIP #5: Shorten Your
Transfer Time by Using Data Compression

As we have mentioned earlier, file sizes have increased dramatically over the years, and this situation definitely affects your communication procedures. The bigger the file, the longer it will take to transfer. In the push for greater speed, on-the-fly data compression and decompression have become an important technology. Figure 8.3 illustrates how data compression can benefit remote communications.

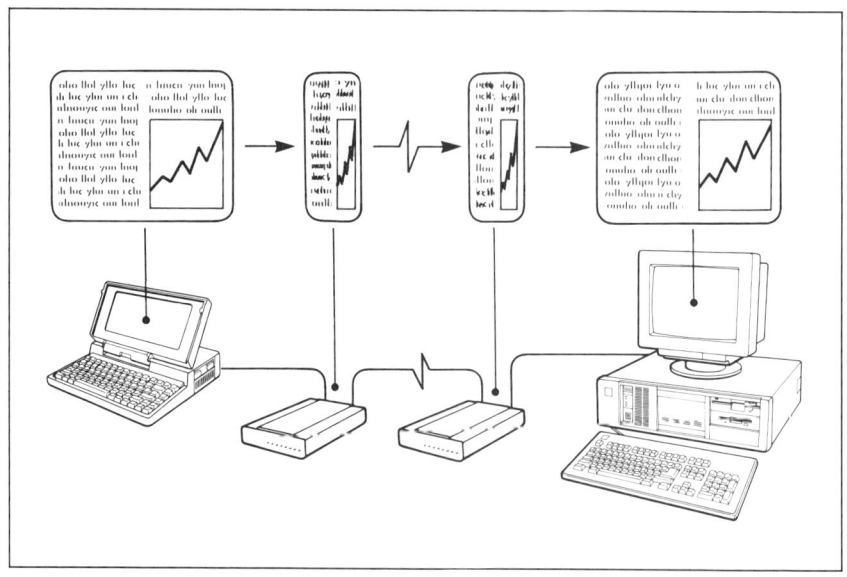

Figure 8.3: Data compression speeds up modem communications

The main data-compression standards are the MNP 5, MNP 7, and V.42bis data-compression protocols. Do not confuse these naming conventions as add-ons to the error-control techniques (MNP 2 through 4 and V.42) mentioned earlier—they operate independently of both error-control and modulation schemes. What this means is that you can purchase a modem with V.42bis data compression built in but without V.42 error-control capabilities. It also means that V.42bis can be found in any modem, from 2400 bps up to 9600 bps.

Data compression can provide a significant increase in transfer performance. The immediate benefit to you will be a reduction in telephone charges. In reality, modems that operate at 2400 bps could have an effective output of 4800 to 8000 bps. This is accomplished in part by the data-buffering methods inherent in MNP 5, MNP 7, and V.42bis, which allow the port speed of your computer to be faster than the signaling rate used between the modems.

Most modem manufacturers design their modems to communicate with the computer at rates up to 9600 bps. Therefore, the way to increase throughput on a 2400-bps modem that has V.42bis capabilities is to configure it to talk with your computer at 9600 bps and the receiving modem at 2400 bps.

In short, a data-compression scheme identifies redundancies or common characters in the data about to be transmitted. It then replaces these items with a significantly shorter data string. The advantage of the speed-buffering technique is there will always be a large amount of information in the queue that can be examined and compressed before it needs to be sent to the receiving modem. Figure 8.4 illustrates how data compression works.

All three compression schemes will compress ASCII and binary data. The way they compress the data is not the same, however, and V.42bis appears to do the best job at this time. The V.42bis scheme uses a tighter compression algorithm (Lempel-Ziv) and it adjusts more quickly to the differences in data flow. On the average, the compression ratios for

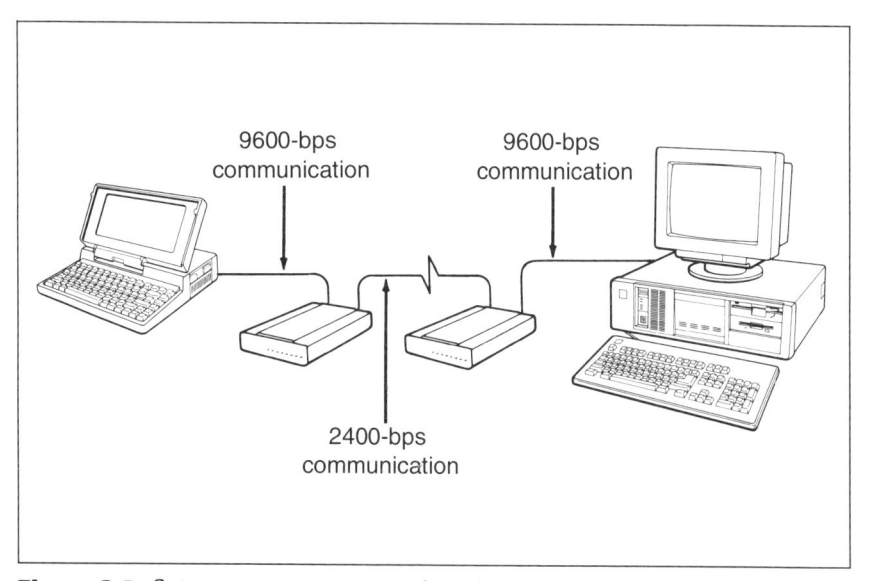

Figure 8.4: Set up your computer and modem to communicate at a higher speed than your modem can communicate with another modem

the three schemes are as follows (file compression varies drastically based on the file type being compressed):

Compression Scheme	Ratio
MNP 5	2:1
MNP 7	3:1
V.42bis	4:1

Our suggestions for a modem set up at 4800 bps or 9600 bps are as follows:

- Disable the bits per second rate adjust. This can be done in most cases by sending the setup string **AT\J0\G0\Q3\N2\V1\%c1.**
- Disable XON\XOFF flow control.

Effective Remote Communications

- Enable bidirectional RTS/CTS.
- Establish a link with the error-control and data-compression schemes.
- Set up the software for the proper port speed.

If you plan on transmitting or receiving files that have already been compressed by a file-compression utility such as PKZIP or Lharc, and your modem has MNP 5 capabilities, make sure that MNP 5 is switched off. The use of MNP 5 while transferring a file that has already been compressed will actually slow down the process. This is because the data must be reanalyzed for potential compression.

Finding the Proper Software Solution

If you already use a communications software package on a desktop machine, the best strategy is to purchase another copy of that package for use on your laptop. Before you make this purchase, however, you should consider two questions:

- Are you going to transfer large amounts of data with a modem that does not have built-in error-control or data-compression capabilities?
- Do you need remote control of another computer?

MODEM SOFTWARE TIP #1: Select Software that Provides Error Control and Data Compression

If your modem does not have error-control or data-compression features built in, you can add these features by selecting the proper software package.

MagicSoft's MTE is a software communication package that creates MNP 4 and 5 protocol support, even though the modem does not have these capabilities. It does not provide the same efficiency as the version built into modems, but it does give you a higher level of error control and data compression than what is available with standard communication packages.

Most popular communication software packages offer error-control and data-compression standards, such as Kermit, XModem, YModem, and ZModem. They may also offer their own proprietary methods as well. For example, DCA's Crosstalk provides Crosstalk and Dart protocols for file transfer with systems using Crosstalk or Crosstalk for Windows.

MODEM SOFTWARE TIP #2: Turn Off Your Software Features If Your Modem Already Has Them

Software-based error-control and data-compression protocols such as XModem operate only during file transfers, while MNP 5 and V.42bis firmware in modems works all the time (if both modems support the protocol).

Transfer rates can be reduced if you are using a modem with MNP 5 or V.42 error control and a communication package that is using another error-control scheme. Therefore, if your laptop has a modem that utilizes MNP 5 or V.42, make sure to select the communication software's no-error-correction option when transferring files. This option is usually accessed through the software's Protocols function or menu option.

MODEM SOFTWARE TIP #3: Use Software that Provides Remote Control of Another Machine

Remote software packages work on the premise that one computer acts as the *host* and the other, in this case your laptop, acts as the *terminal*. For example, you run the package in host mode on your desktop machine and call in from your laptop operating in terminal mode. Your laptop has full control of the desktop machine, including which programs or commands are executed. You issue the commands from your laptop's keyboard and see the results on the screen.

There are software programs that give you the capability to operate another computer from your laptop. Meridian's Carbon Copy and DMA's pcAnywhere are two character-based programs that will allow you to control a computer via remote access. If you want to run Windows

Effective Remote Communications

applications, Horizon Technologies' TechSmith and Ocean Isle's Reach Out are two options.

An added benefit of remote control is that if the host machine can connect to a network or mainframe computer, you can have full access to those connections as well.

However, using a remote-control software package with anything less than a 4800-bps modem will yield unsatisfactory results. Software programs launched on the host machine will appear sluggish and cause frustration if a 2400-bps modem is used. A 9600-bps modem is even better suited to the task of remote control.

Making Sure the Host and Remote Machines Can Communicate

In order to make a successful connection between modems, you must know in advance what software and hardware setup to use. If you are going to have your laptop call your desktop computer, verify all the settings on your desktop before leaving. If you are going to have your laptop call a remote computer, contact the user of the other computer and confirm your settings. Below is a step-by-step approach to help ensure that your laptop will be able to communicate with another computer via modem:

1. Make sure that both modems will be operating with the same settings. These modem settings can be controlled by the communication software packages.

   - The modem is set to work on the same COM port (COM1, COM2, COM3, or COM4) as the software is configured to use.

   - The communication software package has identified the correct brand of modem. Each brand of modem has commands it needs to receive in order to perform an action.

   - The modem is set to the correct speed: from 100 bps to 19,200 bps.

- The modem is set to the correct data bits: 7 or 8.
- The modem is set to the correct parity of odd or even.
- The modem is set to the correct stop bit of 1 or 0.
- The modem is set to the correct flow control of none, XON/XOFF, or RTS/CTS.

2. Make sure that both software communication packages will be using the same terminal settings.

- Terminal types: VT-52, VT-102, VT-200, IBM PC, and so on
- Screen width: 40 columns, 80 columns, or 132 columns
- Auto-line feed: Yes or no
- Enter key: Sends carriage return or carriage return and line feed

3. Make sure that both software communication packages will be using the same transfer protocols.

- CompuServe B
- Kermit
- XModem
- XModem/CRC
- XModem/1K
- YModem
- YModem/Batch
- ZModem
- None (both modems have MNP, V.42, or V.42 and V.42bis error-control and compression capabilities)

4. Make sure that both software communication packages will use the same passwords or IDs when the connection is made.

5. Make sure the host computer's modem is attached to a direct line and not one controlled by a switchboard.

Effective Remote Communications

6. Make sure the software communication package on the host computer is set to answer or auto-answer mode before your laptop calls in.

7. Make sure that your laptop's software communication package will dial the host computer's telephone number properly. Below are some guidelines for dialing out using a software communication package.

- Dialing directly: [telephone#]
- Dialing long distance directly: 1-[area code]-[telephone#]
- Dialing overseas directly: [access]-[country]-[city]-[telephone#]
- Dialing via a 9 line: Precede the number with 9,
- Dialing via an 8 line: Precede the number with 8,
- Dialing via an 8 line and credit card: 8,0-[telephone#],,,,,[credit card#]

In the guidelines above, the dialing codes are represented as follows:

[telephone] The number of the host modem; for example, 555-1212.

[area code] The area code being called; for example, (206).

[access] The long distance carrier's number; for example, AT&T's number is 011.

[country] The number of the country being called. This number can vary from two to three digits; for example, England is 044.

[city] The number of the city being called. The number is not always needed and can vary from one to five digits.

, [comma] For most communication software packages, this causes a 2-second pause before the next set of numbers are transmitted. For example, when using a credit card, you may need 5 to 10 seconds before the card number can be transmitted.

Avoid trying to communicate with an unfamiliar machine while you are under time constraints. Allow 15 to 30 minutes setup time before making the actual connection.

By following the guidelines presented here, you can significantly increase the effectiveness of your remote communications.

NINE

Connecting Your Laptop to a Local Area Network

Because most laptops possess the same CPU as their desktop counterparts, the main networking capability issue is usually connectivity, not processing speed. Depending on your laptop's expansion capabilities, there are five basic hardware options for connecting your laptop to a network:

- A zero-slot connection via a serial or parallel port to a desktop computer that is connected to a network
- Parallel port connection via an external network adapter
- An expansion chassis containing a network interface card
- A proprietary network interface card
- A standard 8-bit or 16-bit network interface card

This chapter describes the alternatives and what you should consider to select the best one for your system.

The Zero-Slot Approach

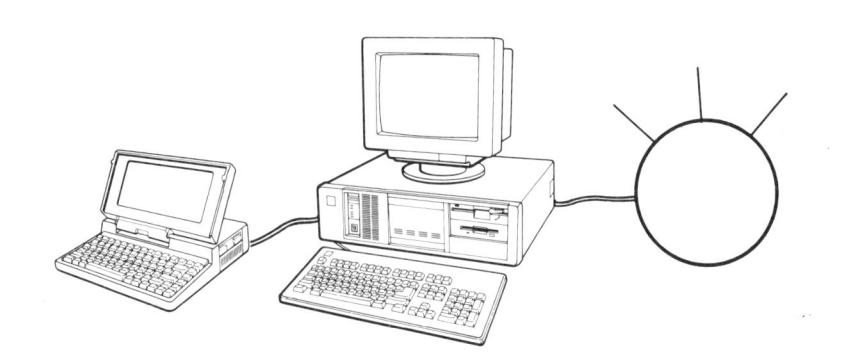

Connecting Your Laptop to a Local Area Network

If your laptop does not have a standard expansion slot and you need access to a LAN, you should consider using a zero-slot LAN package. In this method, the laptop is attached to a computer that has networking capabilities via a serial or parallel port. Through software running on both machines, the laptop has complete access to the other computer. The hard disk on the desktop computer (or *host*) appears as a designated drive (such as D:) on the laptop.

ZERO-SLOT TIP #1: Packages are Inexpensive and Simple to Use

A zero-slot LAN package provides the simplest and least expensive means of attaching your laptop to a network. However, this approach requires control of the desktop computer to work. If the drive names for the network do not conflict with what the laptop expects, your machine will have access to those drives as well. The advantage of a zero-slot package is that it works the same way with any network operating system or cabling scheme. This means your laptop can hook up to any computer on a network and not be affected by the configuration differences between Netware and LAN Manager or Ethernet and ARCnet.

As simple as the zero-slot approach may be, it reaches its limitations quickly. One such limitation is that it does not provide any NetBIOS capabilities. NetBIOS is a standard low-level network interface that many applications need in order to communicate over the network. For example, if your laptop needs access through a client/server application to an SQL database or 3270 terminal emulation—which both require NetBIOS—the zero-slot method is not for you.

Another potential limitation of the zero-slot LAN method is that on average, it performs at one-third the speed of a normal network connection (125 kilobits/second). If your laptop needs to run some high-powered applications, such as a network database program or a graphics package, the performance of a zero-slot package may be unacceptable. Also, the zero-slot method uses RAM on both machines. This overhead reduces the amount of memory available—memory that may be needed to run more powerful programs.

If, however, you just need to transfer some files or run a word processing program, the zero-slot approach will probably be sufficient. There are a number of proven and stable zero-slot LAN packages on the market. Fifth Generation's Brooklyn Bridge, Rupp's Fast Lynx, Software Link's LANLink, and Artisoft's LANtastic /Z are some packages you should consider using.

ZERO-SLOT TIP #2: Answer Some Questions Before Buying a Package

If you need to access a network on an infrequent basis and have the flexibility to take over a desktop computer when doing so, the zero-slot LAN option may be a realistic alternative. A zero-slot approach will be acceptable if you can answer no to all the following questions:

- Do you need access to any network services, such as NetBIOS?
- Will you need to run any large programs, such as a graphics package or network database program?
- Will you need to copy or move large files over the network?
- Will you always have access to a desktop computer that can be devoted exclusively to working with your laptop?
- Will both your laptop and desktop machines need large amounts of RAM to launch a program?

Connecting Your Laptop to a Local Area Network 99

The External LAN Adapter Approach

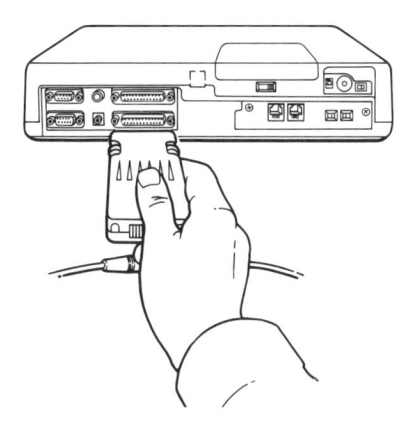

If you need full networking services but your laptop does not have a standard expansion slot or modem slot, you can attach an external LAN adapter to the parallel port of your laptop to make a complete network connection.

You plug one end of the hand-sized adapter into the parallel port of your laptop and attach the other end to a network cable. Each adapter comes with special driver software so that your laptop can connect directly to the LAN.

LAN ADAPTER TIP #1: External Adapters Provide Power in Your Hand

An external LAN adapter can be an excellent option if there are no available standard expansion slots. You should also consider using an external LAN adapter if your laptop needs full-service connections to a variety of network configurations. Carrying three different LAN adapters on a trip is much less cumbersome and provides more flexibility than bringing along three different network cards or an expansion chassis. Hand-sized adapters are priced around $400 to $800.

However, LAN adapters are not very flexible in configuration schemes. Therefore, when making a purchase, you must choose which topology (Ethernet, ARCnet, or Token Ring) and what network operating system (Netware, LAN Manager, etc.) you want as the configuration for the adapter. You will be able to find an adapter to suit most topologies and network operating systems.

Xircom's Pocket LAN Adapter, IQ's PLan adapter, and Meghertz's external adapters are three product lines to consider. We have used these types of adapters with our own laptops and have found their throughput to be about one-half the speed of a normal network connection. Because the technology is fairly new, the adapters do not work with all laptops. One of the original complaints against using an adapter is that laptops lose use of their parallel ports (for local printing) when it is attached. This problem has recently been solved by most manufacturers, who now offer products that provide *pass-through* or *multiplexing* capabilities along with their LAN adapters, so that you can attach to a network and print at the same time.

Another consideration with a network adapter is the need for a wall outlet as a power source. Network adapters do not make use of the laptop for power, and if wall outlets are not readily accessible, your laptop has no means of connecting to the network.

Expansion Chassis: The Expensive Alternative

Connecting Your Laptop to a Local Area Network 101

If your needs for a network connection exist solely at your own desk and your laptop does not have an internal expansion slot, using an expansion chassis is an alternative. A connection to an expansion chassis is made through a special I/O port on the laptop. Not all laptops have the ability to connect to an expansion chassis, so you should check with your laptop manufacturer before purchasing one.

Expansion chassis are expensive ($500 to $1,000) and are not much more than a box with a separate power supply and some expansion (16-bit and 8-bit) slots. The more sophisticated boxes add room for a monitor connection, hard disk drive, and extra serial and parallel ports. If you have an older laptop, some of these additional features could be worthwhile. Newer laptops have most of these features built-in.

Expansion chassis do not have a history of working smoothly. The docking procedure with the laptop does not always work properly, and the connector pins become misaligned, causing connection problems.

As we recommended in Chapter 8, avoid using an expansion chassis if possible. Expansion chassis are meant to operate on your desktop and stay there when you travel with your laptop. Some companies claim expansion chassis are portable. Technically this is correct, but our practical experience has shown otherwise. If you have to connect to a network at a number of locations, an expansion chassis is not an attractive solution.

The Network Interface Card Approach

Another way to give your laptop networking capabilities is through a network interface card. There are two basic types of cards: proprietary and standard.

INTERFACE CARD TIP #1: Proprietary Network Cards Offer Power with No Flexibility

Some laptop manufacturers provide a means to link with networks through customized internal network cards. These proprietary cards fit into an expansion slot of the laptop, leaving the dedicated modem slot open. Third-party manufacturers such as Megahertz and Pure Data take a different approach. They have designed proprietary network cards that work with specific machines by using the laptop's dedicated modem slot.

The major limitation of proprietary network cards is that they rely on special drivers developed by the manufacturers themselves, so only the major topologies and network operating systems are supported. Additionally, if the card connects to the modem slot, you will need an external modem for remote communication.

Because of their relatively high cost (in comparison to the alternatives) and laptop-specific functionality, we recommend that you carefully consider other options before deciding on a proprietary internal network card.

INTERFACE CARD TIP #2: **Standard Network Cards Are the First Choice for Full Connection**

If your laptop has the available slots and you require full networking services, an industry-standard, 16- or 8-bit network interface card should be your first choice for network connections.

Configuration issues are less complicated with a standard interface card. Another benefit of using this type of card is that it will probably be supplied with new software drivers before a proprietary network card or network adapter would get additional drivers.

Getting to Work After Making the Connection

If you are going to connect to an off-site network, do not assume that having the correct hardware will guarantee success. Here are the questions you should ask before going on your trip:

- What network operating system and topology will you be working on?
- What are the proper network shell and device drivers for attaching to the LAN? Do you have them?

Connecting Your Laptop to a Local Area Network

- Should the CONFIG.SYS and AUTOEXEC.BAT files be modified to get onto the network smoothly? If so, how should they be set up?
- How do you get into the system after the hardware has made the connection? Ask for step-by-step instructions.
- Will the default log-in directory, password identification, file, directory, and user group access rights be established before you arrive? If not, who do you contact to set this up? If so, what are they?
- Will your access rights allow you to use network resources such as printers and shared directories?
- Will there be a menu system to work from? If not, ask for the specific locations of programs and files you will need to access. If so, ask for some instruction on how the menu system works.
- What is the proper way to log off the network? Again, get step-by-step instructions if necessary.

Having detailed answers to these questions will ensure that your laptop will work properly on an off-site network.

TEN

Faxing on the Road

When you are traveling with your laptop, bringing or having access to a fax (short for facsimile) device may be essential. It gives you the means to communicate instantly without having to catch people at their telephones or speak quickly into a voice mail system to get your point across.

With a fax machine, you can send and receive contracts, purchase orders, flight schedules, instructions, and any other documents. You can also use a fax device very effectively as a form of electronic mail (called *e-mail*), allowing you to exchange messages with one person or a group of people.

Seasoned travelers know that faxing on the road is not always easy. However, a small amount of planning before your trip can eliminate most of these difficulties. This chapter describes the different types of fax devices available and how to avoid potential faxing pitfalls.

The Fax Machine Alternatives

A fax machine scans a document, converts it into a series of bits (ones and zeros), and send them over a telephone line to a receiving fax machine, which reassembles the bits into a readable image. Since information must be sent over a telephone line, a modem is built into every fax machine. The modem simply converts the bits into a series of tones that can be transmitted over the telephone line.

Even though every fax device has a modem, you cannot necessarily use this modem as you would a standard computer modem, which interfaces with a communication software package. Some fax devices do, however, allow you to use their modem as a standard modem.

You can choose from four main types of fax machines:

- Desktop machines
- Portable, stand-alone devices
- Internal boards
- Pocket-size, serial-port devices

The following sections describe the advantages and disadvantages of using the various types of fax machines while you are away from your home base.

FAX TYPE TIP #1: Use Desktop Fax Machines to Send Hard Copies

Desktop fax machines sit on a desk or table and allow you to send and receive documents to and from any other fax device. Their main advantage is that they use paper, so you can fax any type of hard-copy (paper) documents, such as contracts, brochures, and purchase orders. For example, if a customer hands you a ten-page contract, you can use a desktop machine to fax it to your home office immediately. The more expensive units have a wide range of features, such as a paper feeder for sending multipage documents and higher transmission speeds.

Here is a summary of the advantages of desktop fax machines:

- They work with hard-copy documents.
- Most hotels, conference centers, and companies have desktop fax machines, so you can almost always find one.
- You do not have to buy anything for your laptop, because you can use the fax machine available at your location.
- Some units offer a wide range of features.

The disadvantages of desktop fax machines are as follows:

- They are not portable.
- You cannot fax a document produced on your laptop without printing it first.
- The location of the machine you can use may not be convenient.

FAX TYPE TIP #2: Portable, Stand-Alone Fax Machines Are Not That Portable

Portable, stand-alone fax machines are similar to desktop fax units, but they are smaller and can be carried on the road. As with desktop machines, the major advantage of portable, stand-alone devices is that they can handle documents in paper form. However, portable fax machines usually do not have the features that the better desktop units include. For example, most portable machines do not have page-feeding capabilities. Their portability is somewhat of an illusion as well, and you will get tired of lugging them around in addition to your laptop.

In summary, the advantage of portable, stand-alone fax machines is that they can handle hard-copy documents. Their disadvantages are as follows:

- They are bulky to carry.
- You cannot fax a document produced on your laptop without printing it.
- They require more maintenance than fax boards or serial-port devices.
- They are more expensive than fax-modem boards or serial-port fax modems.

FAX TYPE TIP #3: Internal Fax-Modem Boards Are the Choice for the Frequent Traveler

Internal fax-modem boards plug into an expansion slot inside a desktop or laptop computer. In a laptop, some plug into a standard 8- or 16-bit slot, and others plug into the proprietary slot. Although combined fax-modem boards are more expensive than the other fax devices, they make the most sense for the laptop user who travels often. They provide two capabilities while taking only one of your laptop's slots, and they eliminate the need to carry other external devices.

Faxing on the Road

The following are the main advantages of internal fax or fax-modem boards:

- They send and receive documents in electronic form from any telephone.
- You do not have to carry an extra device (or forget to take it).
- They require almost no maintenance.
- They provide both a fax and a modem in one unit.
- Their text and graphics output quality is much better than that of stand-alone units, because you can send the output to a laser printer (which supports higher resolution).

The disadvantages of internal fax boards are as follows:

- They cannot send or produce hard copies.
- It is difficult to use them for both your laptop and desktop computers because of the installation requirements. If the board fits into a proprietary laptop slot (which many do), it cannot be installed in a desktop computer.
- They use the laptop battery source for power.

FAX TYPE TIP #4: Pocket-Size, Serial-Port Devices Pack Functionality into a Small Space

Pocket-size, serial-port fax-modem devices are about the size of a deck of cards and plug directly into one of your laptop's serial ports. They generally provide the same capabilities as internal fax-modem boards, without having to be installed internally.

The key advantages of these pocket-sized devices are as follows:

- They allow you to send and receive documents in electronic form anywhere, anytime.
- They perform as a fax and a modem.

- You can move them from your desktop to your laptop computer because they are easy to install and remove.
- They do not take up a slot inside your laptop.
- Many come with their own battery (standard 9-volt alkaline), which saves your laptop's battery power.
- They provide better text and graphics output quality than stand-alone units, because you can print their output on laser printers.
- Most provide LED (light-emitting diode) readouts showing the transmission speed and carrier-detect signal, so you can see activity on the line. (Internal fax boards do not have LED readouts.)

Pocket-size, serial-port fax devices have the following disadvantages:

- They cannot send or produce hard copies
- Although they are very small, they are still an extra device you must carry around.

And the Winner Is . . .

Overall, it is hard to beat the pocket-size, serial port fax-modem devices in terms of flexibility, convenience, and ease of use. We have used Touchbase Systems' WorldPort 2496 with good results. This product provides both 2400-bps modem and 9600-bps Group III facsimile capabilities.

Internal fax-modem boards are also a good choice for most laptop users. We suggest that you stay away from portable, stand-alone fax machines unless you really need to transmit hard copies while on the road.

If you buy a serial-port fax-modem device for your laptop, get one that fits into the proprietary (nonstandard) slot, and leave the standard (AT-compatible) slot free for other uses. Fax modems designed for proprietary slots are specific to each laptop model, so you should check with your laptop manufacturer to see which type is suitable for your machine. If you decide to purchase a fax modem that fits into a standard slot in your laptop, we recommend Intel's SatisFAXtion device.

Fax Features for Travelers

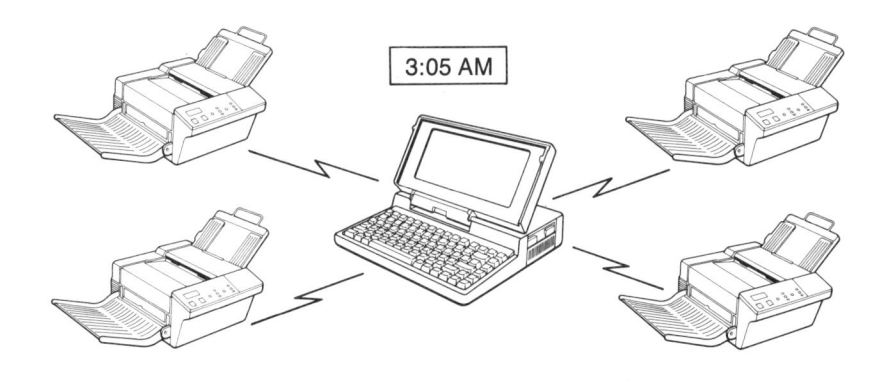

Not having the right fax features at a critical time on the road can result in frustration and lost business. If you travel and fax frequently, it pays to have a better device with a full range of features. The following sections describe some of the features that your fax should have.

FAX FEATURE TIP #1: Fax While You Sleep

A fax device with *scheduled transmission* allows you to send a fax at a designated time of day. This can be a real money-saver on the road because you can set a time for your fax to transmit late at night or before sunrise to take advantage of low telephone rates. This is especially important for faxing from hotels, some of which have a 10 to 30 percent surcharge added to the normal telephone company rates.

Also, you do not have to be at your computer to send a fax that must be received at a certain time, perhaps for a meeting being held in another time zone.

FAX FEATURE TIP #2: Broadcast Your Messages

Some devices have the capability to broadcast faxes, which means that you can compose a document on your laptop and send it to dozens of different fax machines automatically. Most fax boards do this through software that comes with the board. The software allows you to store frequently called fax numbers in a directory. From the directory, you create a "distribution list" of people who you want to receive the fax, and your software and fax board do the rest.

Broadcasting capability is especially important if you need to keep in touch with many people while on the road but can't find the time to keep calling everyone. You simply compose a single document (perhaps a trip status report) using your favorite word processor, and then broadcast it to as many people as you like.

FAX FEATURE TIP #3: Fax with the Ease of Printing

Printer redirection is a feature that gives you the ability to "print" documents to your fax board. Through special software supplied with the fax board, you can convert Epson, Hewlett-Packard (HP) LaserJet, or PostScript output to Group III fax format from within your applications. In this manner, faxing is almost as easy as printing from an application.

For laptop users, printer redirection is a critical feature because it eliminates the need to find a printer when you want to fax a document you just created in WordPerfect, Word, Excel, 1-2-3, or another application. Note that most manufacturers provide this feature only in non-Windows environments.

Faxing on the Road with Desktop Units

If you don't bring your faxing capabilities with you when you travel, you'll have to use one of the millions of fax machines that are in service around the world. But don't assume that since there are so many of them that you'll be able to find one easily. Also, if you need to fax something that you've produced on your laptop, you will need to print it first.

DESKTOP FAXING TIP #1:
Check the Availability of the Machine

Before you leave, call ahead to the hotels where you'll be staying and ask about their faxing capabilities. Virtually all the four- and five-star hotels have fax machines that can be used by guests, but some of the three-star hotels do not. For an additional charge, some of the five-star hotels will even supply a fax machine in your room if you request it in advance.

Many private postal box companies also have fax devices that you can use. For example, nearly all Mail Boxes Etc offices have fax machines. Again, call before you leave and make sure you have access to a few different options.

At night, finding a fax machine is much more difficult. This is when you must rely on the better hotels to provide 24-hour fax service for you.

DESKTOP FAXING TIP #2: Know Where You Will Print

If you are going to fax documents with a desktop fax machine, you will need to use a printer to produce hard copies of the documents before you fax them. Along with planning which fax machine you will use, you should also arrange your access to a printer (laser or dot-matrix) before you leave on your trip. While finding a fax machine is not too difficult, finding a printer can be a hassle.

Most hotels will fax documents for you, but they won't do your printing. Only at some of the better hotels (the ones with "business centers") will you find laser printing capabilities. A few copier stores (such as Kinkos) have Apple laser printers that you can rent for a per-page fee, but you need to connect your laptop directly to the printer and reconfigure it to drive an Apple LaserWriter. Another option is to go to the nearest large computer store (such as Businessland) and ask one of the employees to print your document.

Faxing on the Road with a Portable Fax Machine

With a portable, stand-alone fax machine, the two major issues are printing documents produced on your laptop and adapting your unit to the telephone requirements of your particular location.

Just as when you will be using a desktop fax machine, you must make sure that you have access to an appropriate printer so that you can produce hard copies to transmit. See the previous section for suggestions on locating a printer.

Adapting to your location's telephone requirements can also be a problem. You might find, for example, that the telephone jack is *hard-wired* (not modular), and therefore there is no standard jack in which to plug your fax unit. In these cases, you must use an acoustic coupler to attach directly to the handset of a telephone. See Chapter 11 for more information about acoustic couplers.

Faxing on the Road with an Internal or Serial-Port Device

When you use either an internal fax board or an external, serial-port fax, you have four primary concerns:

- Adapting to the telephone-wiring requirements at each location
- Getting a stable telephone line with little or no static
- Finding a way to fax hard copies
- Making sure that your software can output images that the fax device can handle

The first two problems are addressed in Chapter 11. The following sections provide some tips for faxing hard copies and getting your applications to interface properly with your fax device.

Faxing on the Road **115**

INTERNAL OR SERIAL-PORT FAXING TIP #1:
Hand-Held Scanners Provide Hard Copies on the Spot

If you will be faxing hard copies on the road with moderate frequency (several times per trip) and you cannot predict your access to a desktop fax machine, consider purchasing a hand-held scanner. These devices typically scan one-half page at a time, and they come with software that helps you align the two halves into a full page. You can save the image in TIFF, PCX, and other formats that most fax-board software can accept. They are reasonably small, cost less than $200, and easily fit into a briefcase or suitcase. You can also use the same scanner with your desktop computer.

Note that a hand-held scanner is not practical for longer documents. For a 30-page contract, for example, a desktop fax machine is the only way to go. However, for faxes that average 2 to 5 pages, a hand-held scanner can make life on the road much easier.

Some fax-modem boards even come with a scanner interface built into them. Intel's SatisFAXtion is one such board, and it is highly rated.

Two scanners that we recommend are the Marstek M800 and Logitech's Scanman Model 32. Before you buy a scanner, check with your fax manufacturer to see which file formats are acceptable to your fax device, and then shop for a scanner that can save files in those formats.

We recommend hand-held scanners over portable fax machines because they are smaller; allow you to capture hard-copy text and graphics into electronic format; and can be used for many other purposes besides faxing, such as transferring photographs and other graphics into your application.

INTERNAL OR SERIAL-PORT FAXING TIP #2:
Use Printer Redirection to Send Formatted Documents

It may be important for the document you fax to retain its formatting. When you fax a document directly from your laptop, it might not arrive in the same format in which it left. How do you fax a document created in WordPerfect, Excel, 1-2-3, or another program so that it looks as if you had printed it first and then faxed the printed hard copy?

Some fax boards and external pocket devices cannot send faxes with any formatting at all. Others require you to first convert the document to ASCII (plain text) or PCX file format before sending it. The problem with ASCII format is that most of your document's original formatting will be lost. With PCX, the problem is that many word processing applications cannot read the file because it is in graphics format, not standard text format.

Some fax-modem products, however, allow you to fax output as it appears on the printer. Typically, this is done either through *printer redirection* or by *printer capture*. With printer capture, the fax software operates either in the background, capturing output normally directed to a printer, or works directly with printer output that has been redirected to a file instead of the printer port. The output is usually in Epson 9-pin format, which is easily converted to Group III fax format.

We do not recommend setting up your fax modem for background printer capture because this means the software must operate as a TSR (terminate-and-stay-resident) program. TSRs have a reputation for causing memory conflicts with other applications (often causing your system to fail). The best method is to use your application to direct the printer output to a file instead of to the printer port. Figure 10.1 illustrates how printer redirection works.

With DOS applications, the procedure to send printer output to a file will differ depending on the application. Consult your software's documentation to see how to redirect your printer output to a file. Also, consult your fax documentation to see which printer output it supports. Typically, fax devices support HP LaserJet and Epson 9-pin formats.

If you are working with Windows applications, which all use the same set of printer drivers, you can use the following procedure to redirect printer output to a file so that it can be converted by your fax-modem software and sent as a fax image:

1. Check to see if a Windows printer driver that your fax device supports is installed. This will be either HP LaserJet or, more commonly, Epson 9-pin. Check your fax documentation to see which driver is supported.

Faxing on the Road 117

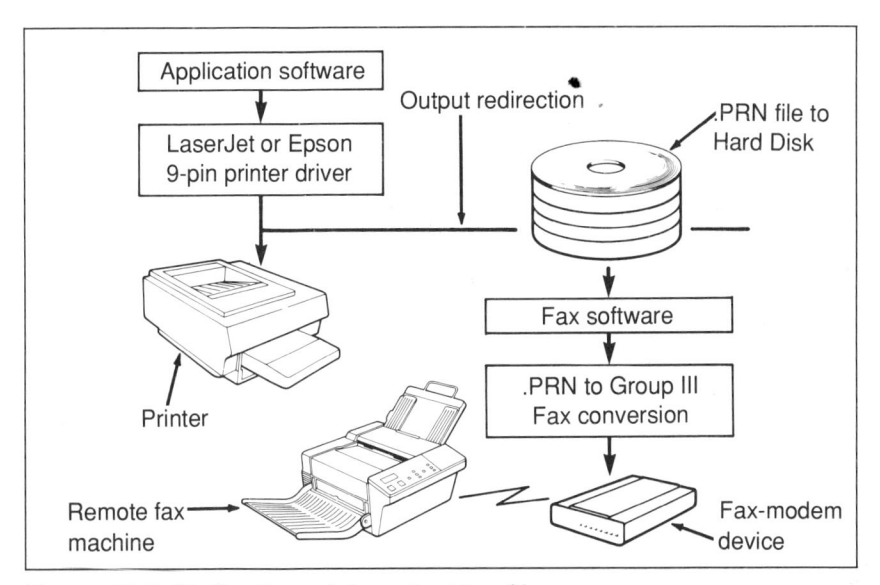

Figure 10.1: Redirecting printer output to a file

- Open the Windows Control Panel in the Main program group.
- In the window that appears, select the Printers icon, and then examine the list of printers already installed.
- If the appropriate printer driver is not listed, select the Add Printer button, select the correct printer device, and then choose Install. Windows will prompt you to insert the printer driver disk in one of your disk drives and will copy the driver onto your hard disk. Once the appropriate printer driver is displayed in the list of installed printers, select that driver, and then select the Configure option button.
- In the dialog box that pops up, select FILE: as the output port. This will direct that printer driver to prompt you for a file name each time you print from a Windows application. Remember that selecting this printer will always send output

to a file, and you must reconfigure your printer to the appropriate port when you want to direct your output back to your printer.

- Make sure that the printer driver is active by selecting the printer driver and then selecting the Active radio button. Finally, select the OK button to exit.

2. From any Windows application, open a document, then select File and Print. You will be prompted to input a file name. Consult your fax device's documentation for appropriate file names. They usually end with the extension .PRN. The document will be sent to disk in a format that your fax device understands.

3. You can now run your fax software and specify this file as a fax to send. Some fax devices (such as Touchbase's WorldPort 2496 fax modem) automatically convert PRN files to Group III fax format. Other devices require that you first convert the file to Group III fax format with a special utility before you send it.

In this manner, you can fax formatted documents from virtually all Windows applications, including Word for Windows, Excel, 1-2-3, and even PageMaker.

INTERNAL OR SERIAL-PORT FAXING TIP #3:
ASCII Format Works with Most Faxes

If your fax device does not support standard printer output, another option is to send plain ASCII text. Virtually all fax devices take ASCII text files as direct input. This is also a good fall-back option when you cannot figure out how to send an application-specific file format (such as Word-Perfect), or the transmission does not seem to be working properly.

First, open the file you want to send (such as a Word document or a 1-2-3 spreadsheet) and save it in ASCII file format. Then, with most fax devices, you just start your fax software and type in the name of the ASCII file you want to send. Although the converted document loses most of its formatting characteristics (such as bold, italics, underlines, and different typefaces), you can at least transmit the text portion of the data. See Chapter 4 for more information about ASCII files.

INTERNAL OR SERIAL-PORT FAXING TIP #4:
Some Devices Work with Graphics

Some fax modems have the capability to send files containing graphics or both text and graphics. Usually, you must use your application to convert the file format to PCX, TIFF, or some other standard graphics format. Consult your fax-modem documentation to see which file format is supported, and see Chapter 4 for more information about converting files from within your applications.

Most word processing packages cannot convert files to PCX because they do not support graphics formats. However, you can use a graphics package such as Corel Draw or Windows Paintbrush (both of which support PCX) to create a graphics file that can be sent along with the original text file.

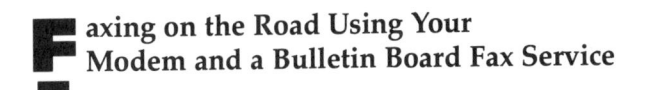

Faxing on the Road Using Your Modem and a Bulletin Board Fax Service

---

XYZ Bulletin Board Service

What type of message do you wish to send?

1. E-Mail
2. Fax

Enter your choice: 2
What is the fax number: 555-5512
What is the file you wish to upload and send? C:\FAXMEMO.DOC

****Your message has been accepted and properly routed****

If you don't want to invest the money in a fax device for your laptop and finding a desktop fax machine is impractical, another viable option is to use a fax service provided by MCI, Compuserve, or another bulletin board service. A wide variety of telecommunications programs support faxing through a bulletin board service.

All you need is a modem and an account on any bulletin board service that supports fax routing—you do not need a fax device. Using your modem, connect to the bulletin board service in the standard way. Select the fax option when the bulletin board service menu appears on your screen. When prompted, supply the number of the fax device to which you want to transmit the file. Then choose an ASCII text file on your disk (or some other file format supported by the bulletin board service). The file will be uploaded to the service, and from there it will be sent to the fax number you specified.

Receiving Faxes on the Road

When you receive a fax while you are on the road, you may need to incorporate it in a document. Because your fax device receives the fax in Group III facsimile format, first you will need to convert it into another format, which requires a special utility.

Another potential problem with receiving faxes is running out of space on your disk. Group III facsimile files can be quite large.

The following sections provide some suggestions for transferring your faxes into your documents, as well as how to handle disk storage of the faxes you receive.

FAX RECEIPT TIP #1: Convert the Fax to PCX to Bring It into a Document

The usual method for incorporating fax images into your documents is to use a fax software utility to convert the Group III fax format into a popular file format, usually PCX. Since a fax is nothing more than a graphic image consisting of a series of bits, there is no practical method

Faxing on the Road 121

for converting it into text that you can incorporate into your documents. Some applications let you place a PCX image directly into the document, but the fax image must be small (usually no more than one page) in order for your system to have enough memory to perform the copy operation. Exit as many applications as you can and close all DOS terminal sessions before you try this.

If you use Windows, the best way to manipulate fax images in PCX format is with Windows Paintbrush or some other graphics application that lets you edit PCX images. To edit a PCX file with Paintbrush, follow these steps:

1. Select the Edit menu option, then select Paste From.

2. In the dialog box that appears, click on the PCX radio button to select PCX format, and then open the PCX image on disk.

3. The image should appear in the Paintbrush Window. You can now manipulate the image by using Paintbrush's many features. For instance, you can shrink or expand the image and reverse the video. Consult your Windows documentation for more information about using Paintbrush.

4. When you are finished editing the image, select the cutting tool (the little scissors picture in the tool bar) and mark the portion of the fax image you want to export to your Windows application.

5. Select Edit from the main Paintbrush menu, then select Copy.

6. Close the Paintbrush application (to free memory that you might need for the copy operation), start your word processor, and open the document you want to import the image into.

7. From your application's main menu, select Edit, then select Paste.

The fax image should appear in you application window. For more information about importing graphic images, consult your application's documentation.

FAX RECEIPT TIP #2: Compress Your Fax Files

Fax images can take an enormous amount of space on your disk. Group III fax images of fine (200 × 200 lines per inch) and superfine (200 × 400 lines per inch) resolution can take between 20K to 100K *per page*, depending on the number of shades of gray supported.

If you plan on receiving faxes regularly on your laptop, you should have a good compression utility such as PKZIP. Better still, you should have a professional tools package, such as Central Point Software's PC Tools or Symantec's The Norton Utilities, which allows you to compress these images and back them up on floppy disks in one step.

ELEVEN

Working in Hostile Environments

Wherever you take your laptop, a variety of factors can turn the workplace into a hostile environment. The best strategy is to assume that your next laptop workplace will provide you with many challenges. This chapter offers suggestions for overcoming even the most adverse conditions.

Call-Ahead Check List

Your best protection in a hostile environment is to plan ahead. Determine the exact locations where you will want to work on your computer. Then call and confirm what environment is going to be provided for you and your laptop. Some of the questions to ask include the following:

- Is there a desktop area that will be large enough to accommodate both the machine and its accessories?

- Is there a wall plug with enough outlets to meet the power needs for your laptop and accessories? How close are these outlets to the desktop area?

- Is there a telephone wall jack within reach of the desktop? Is it a direct line or controlled by a switchboard? Is the line hard-wired to a telephone or does it have a modular telephone jack (RJ-11)?

- What type of lighting is available? Is there direct sunlight? If so, can it be controlled by shades, curtains, or blinds?

- Is there a computer printer nearby that can be used? If so, what type is it and how is it connected (to the computer's serial or parallel port)?

- Is there a computer network that can be used? If so, what do you need to connect to it? (See Chapter 9 for a list of questions to ask if a network is available.)

Working in Hostile Environments

If it is not possible for you to call ahead, you will just have to be prepared for the worst. The tips in the remainder of this chapter will give you an idea of what situations you may encounter.

Taking Control in Hotel/Motel Rooms

Hotel and motel rooms were not designed with laptop computers in mind. (Some would argue that they were not designed with travelers in mind either, but that is a subject for a different book). As shown in Figure 11.1, the standard hotel room has three electrical outlets in the living area: one outlet by the table near the window, one by the nightstand between the two standard double-sized beds, and one below the writing desk portion of a bureau. Any additional outlets will be located in the bathroom area. Few hotel rooms offer more than three outlets.

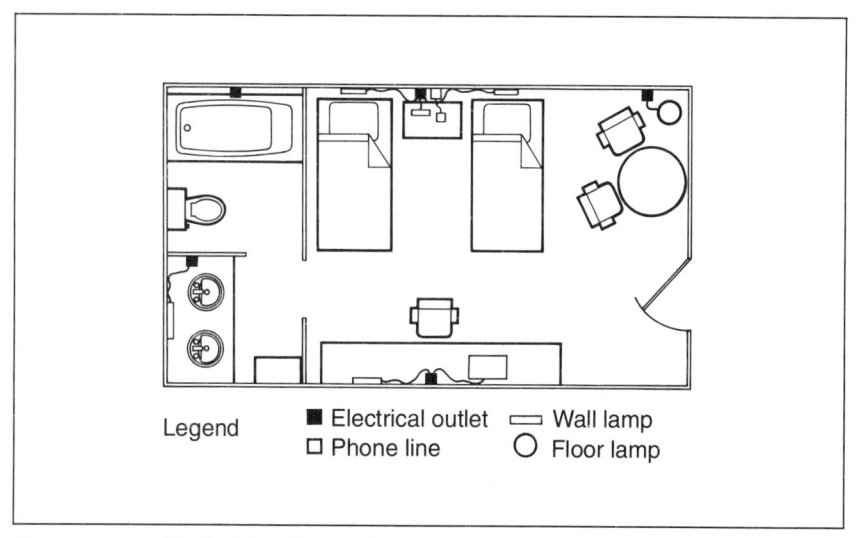

Figure 11.1: Typical hotel room layout

The wall plug nearest to the table by the window will, in most cases, have two outlets. One outlet is usually used by a floor lamp and the second outlet (in older motels) is often used by an air conditioner.

The wall plug behind the nightstand (often inaccessible) will probably have four outlets. Two outlets may be used by wall lamps near each bed. The third outlet may be used by a table lamp on the nightstand. The fourth will be used by a radio/alarm clock.

The wall plug nearest the bureau (often inaccessible) will usually have two outlets. The first will be used by a lamp. The second will be used by the television set.

For the most part, each electrical outlet is being used by some device. What this means to you is that some device in the room will have to be disconnected in order for you to use your laptop.

We have found that the outlet near the table by the window is the most likely location for your computer connection. The advantage here is that it will be closest to the largest workspace area. The disadvantages are that this workspace is the farthest away from a telephone jack, and the wall plug may have the smallest number of outlets. Also, if the curtains do not work properly, outside light may make it difficult to read your laptop's video display.

HOTEL/MOTEL TIP #1: Bring Along the Proper Battle Gear

By calling ahead and asking the questions from our check list and bringing the proper battle gear (see Chapter 1), working with your laptop in a hotel or motel room can be tolerable. Most often, the best solution is to bring a longer telephone cable and a grounded wall plug with an adapter that provides more outlets and a surge protector. This way, you will not have to work from one of the beds or disconnect any of the electrical devices.

Hooking Up to a Telephone

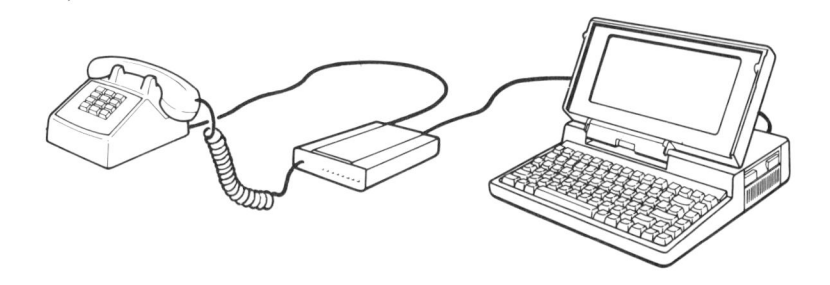

In Chapters 1, 8, and 10, we discussed the various ways to optimize remote communications on a laptop. While traveling, you may find some situations in which making any connection at all is difficult.

TELEPHONE HOOKUP TIP #1: Bring a Communications Kit

If you travel frequently with your laptop, need remote communication capabilities, and the types of communication hookups will vary from site to site, you will need to take some tools with you. Here are the items that we recommend:

- A communications toolkit that includes a small screwdriver, magnifying glass, and small flashlight.
- A device that will let your modem work with digital telephone systems that require special data jacks or with hard-wired telephones (see the next tip for details).
- An acoustic coupling device that will work with pay telephones or foreign telephone systems, such as the Telecoupler, which is available from Computer Products Plus or most Radio Shack stores.

Using acoustic couplers is the least preferable method because their connections are more sensitive to noise and static than connections made directly through a modem.

TELEPHONE HOOKUP TIP #2: Use a Device to Connect to Any Telephone

If you use your modem in hostile environments, you should purchase a device that will allow you to connect your modem to any type of telephone, such as CP+ Connection from Computer Products Plus, or Konnexx from Unlimited Systems, which is illustrated in Figure 11.2. Such devices cost about $100. Look for a device with the following features:

- Automatic voice/data recognition (or manual switching), which turns off the telephone's handset microphone in data mode, so that noise does not interfere with data transmission

- Automatic or manual polarity switching, which can compensate for the wiring differences of telephone systems (most often occurring in hotels and motels)

- An adapter that will allow the connection device to work with a hard-wired telephone

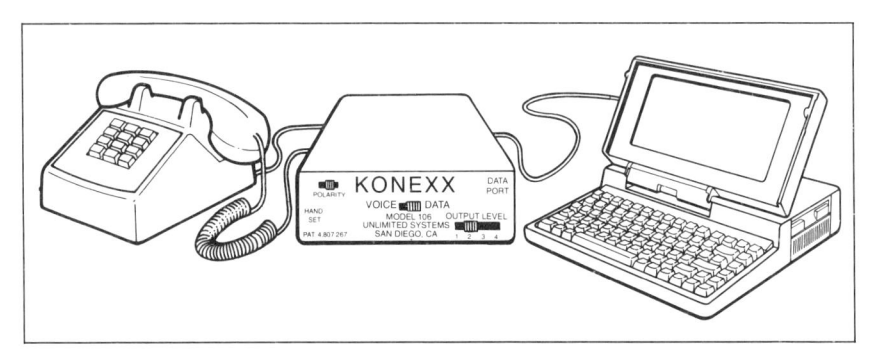

Figure 11.2: A Konnexx device hooks up your modem to a telephone

Working in Hostile Environments

To make a connection using a device such as Konnexx or CP+ Connection, follow this procedure:

1. Make the physical connection.

   - Remove the modular plug at the end of the coiled handset cord that is attached to the telephone.
   - Plug the connection device's handset cable into the empty jack on the telephone.
   - Plug the coiled handset cord into the connection device's jack (most likely marked *Handset*).
   - Plug the cable from the modem's line jack into the connection device's modem jack (most likely marked *Data*).

2. Start your communication.

   - Set up your laptop's modem and communication software to dial, but do not start the actual dialing.
   - Get a dial tone by picking up the handset.
   - Have the computer start dialing.
   - Confirm that you want the connection to be made.
   - Lay down the handset until the communication is complete.

Working in Airports

One of the most hostile work environments for a laptop user can be the airport terminal, where you are often forced to sit through flight delays. Laptop users are tempted to use this time to work on their computers. Unfortunately, airport work areas suitable for you and your laptop are rare.

AIRPORT TIP #1: Find a Work Area

Before you travel, do some research on the airports you will be going through. Many major airports provide business centers that supply work areas and other resources (such as fax machines) to laptop users. The Official Airline Guide (OAG) offers a set of databases called the OAG Electronic Edition Travel Service. One of its databases, called Nationwide Intelligence, provides complete background information on most of the airports in the United States. See Chapter 12 for more information about the OAG database system.

Some airline clubs provide computer work areas within airports. The availability of work space varies from airline to airline and airport to airport. If you travel often, check with the airlines you use the most to see what types of work areas their clubs offer. For the annual cost of a club membership, you may gain valuable work hours.

Other than business centers or airline clubs, here are some other options for airport work areas:

- Find restaurants or lounges that have tabletops you can work on. Do not abuse your right to use the workspace. If the restaurant or lounge is crowded, find another work area.

- Find parts of the terminal that have electrical outlets and are used on an infrequent basis. For example, some airline gates are used only once or twice a day by charter airlines.

AIRPORT TIP #2: Get Through Airport Security Safely

The effect of x-ray and metal-detection machines on computer equipment is unpredictable. Some computer users claim that these machines have never caused a problem, while others hold them responsible for the loss of many megabytes of data. Our position is that your data is too valuable to take any chances. When you are taking your laptop through airport security, it is always best to hand it to the security agent on the other side of the security barrier. Keep your laptop away from *both* x-ray and metal-detection devices.

Working in Hostile Environments

Another simple precaution is to take floppy disks and cartridge tapes out of your carry-on bags before you pass the bags through the airport security machine. Hand the disks, tapes, and your laptop to the security agent.

TWELVE

Extra Tips for You and Your Laptop

This chapter contains suggestions for transferring data between incompatible floppy disk drives, conserving your laptop's battery power, and backing up your data while traveling. It also describes some computerized information resources that are designed for frequent travelers.

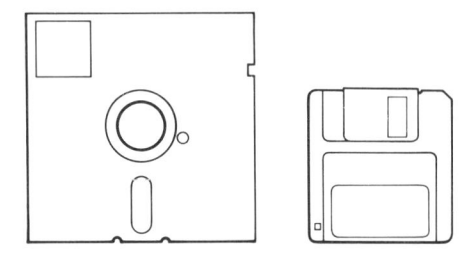

Floppy Disk Drive Compatibility

On the road, you are likely to encounter a wide range of computer configurations. The easiest way to exchange information with other computers is through the use of floppy disks. You simply copy a file from your hard disk to a floppy disk and hand the floppy disk to someone who puts it into his or her computer and copies the file onto the hard disk.

However, floppy disk exchange does not always work this smoothly. The most important point to remember is that not every computer has the same type of floppy disk drive. There are many different combinations of disk drives. Here are the more common ones:

- 5¼-inch drive sizes:
    - 360K double-sided, double-density
    - 1.2MB double-sided, high-density
- 3½-inch drive sizes:
    - 720K double-sided, double-density
    - 1.44MB double-sided, high-density

Extra Tips for You and Your Laptop   **135**

There are also single-sided versions of these drives (with lower capacities), but these are uncommon.

Most floppy disk labels indicate the disk's type. Typically, the letter designation *DD* on the disk label stands for double-sided, double-density and indicates 720K capacity on a 3½-inch disk, or 360K capacity on a 5¼-inch disk. If the label has the designation *HD*, it usually is a high-density disk, with 1.44MB capacity on a 3½-inch disk, or 1.2MB capacity on a 5¼-inch disk.

When you are on the road and someone hands a floppy disk to you, will your laptop be able to read the disk? If you are giving someone a disk, will his or her machine support that capacity or size? The following sections provide examples of the various points you should consider for floppy disk data transfers.

FLOPPY DRIVE TIP #1: The Disk with the Data You Want to Import May Not Be Compatible with Your Laptop

On your journeys with your laptop, you may encounter one of the following situations:

- *Scenario 1: Your laptop's floppy drive supports a higher storage capacity than the disk you want to read.* This is not a problem. Floppy disk drives are "upward compatible," which means that a disk formatted in a lower capacity can be read by a drive that supports a higher capacity. Therefore, 720K floppy disks can be inserted into a drive that supports the 1.44MB format.

- *Scenario 2: Your laptop's floppy drive supports a lower capacity than the disk you want to read.* This can be a problem. Floppy drives are not "downward compatible." They cannot read information from disks that were formatted by a higher capacity drive. If, for example, your laptop has a 720K drive and you have just been handed a 1.44MB disk, you will need to request that the disk be formatted in a 720K capacity (or less) before your computer can read it. Since higher capacity drives can format diskettes in capacities lower than they support, this is a reasonable request.

- *Scenario 3: You have just been handed a 5¼-inch diskette and your laptop's drive is 3½-inch.* In this case, you will need to request a 3½-inch diskette or use a communication program such as LapLink to transfer files directly from one hard disk to another or from the hard disk of the originating computer to a floppy disk.

FLOPPY DRIVE TIP #2: **The Disk with the Data You Want to Export May Not Be Compatible with the Other Computer**

If you want to give someone a floppy disk created on your laptop's floppy drive, consider the following scenarios:

- *Scenario 1: The computer that is to read a disk from your laptop's floppy drive supports a higher capacity.* This is not a problem. As explained in the previous tip, a drive of a higher capacity can always read a disk formatted in a lower capacity.

- *Scenario 2: The computer that is to read a disk from your laptop's floppy drive supports a lower capacity.* This is not a problem either. Using the MS-DOS FORMAT command on your laptop, format a blank diskette in the capacity supported by the computer that will read the diskette. For example, if your laptop has a 1.44MB drive with the device letter A, and the computer that will read your diskette has a 720K floppy drive, format the diskette in your laptop with the command FORMAT A: /F 720K. If your laptop's floppy drive has a different device letter (such as B), use that letter instead. The /F: 720K parameter formats the diskette as a 720K diskette.

- *Scenario 3: You want to transfer files to a computer that has only a 5¼-inch disk drive.* In this case, you will need to use a communications program such as LapLink to transfer files directly from one hard disk to another.

Prolonging the Life of Your Laptop's Batteries

Most laptop manufacturers quote battery life as "2 to 3 hours." In critical situations, the difference between 2 and 3 hours is substantial. Why are battery lifetimes so indefinite and what can be done to take maximum advantage of them?

The answer to these questions lies mostly in the way your laptop consumes power. Of all the components within your laptop, there are three major consumers of power:

- Your hard disk drive
- Your floppy drive
- Your screen

Since your hard disk and floppy drives are mechanical systems, they require more power for operation than purely electronic components. Your laptop screen also requires a relatively large amount of battery power, but different types of screens have different power requirements. Gas plasma and electroluminescent screens typically generate the most light and heat, and therefore use more power. LCD (liquid crystal display) technology uses less power, but manufacturers provide backlighting to make the screens more readable in different lighting conditions, which consumes additional power.

As suggested in Chapter 1, one way to ensure that you will not run out of battery power while traveling is to take an extra battery pack with you. This other battery pack can be a lifesaver on an airplane flight that has lasted longer than your laptop's power supply. However, whether you are on the road or at your office, it is always wise to conserve your laptop's battery power. The following sections provide suggestions for prolonging the life of your laptop's batteries.

BATTERY SAVING TIP #1: Lower Your Screen's Light Output

The amount of power a laptop's screen consumes is related to how much light it has to generate. If every pixel on your screen is displayed at its highest intensity, it consumes large amounts of power. To reduce the power requirements of your screen, minimize the amount of light given off by your display while maintaining its readability.

For example, Toshiba laptop users running Windows can take the following steps to adjust their screen settings:

1. Start Windows and click twice on the Control Panel icon, which is usually located in the group labeled Main.

2. Click twice on the Color icon, and then click on the down arrow to the right of the Color Scheme drop-down list box. A number of preset Windows color schemes will appear.

3. Select the Fluorescent color scheme.

4. Click on the Color Palette button.

5. Change Window Background to the fifth color in the fifth column.

6. Change Window Text to the bottom-right color (white).

7. Change Application Workspace to the second color in the last column.

8. Click on the Save Scheme button, and then click on OK to save your changes.

Some laptop manufacturers recommend optimal color selections for their screens. If you cannot find a list of these settings in your laptop documentation, call the manufacturer. If the manufacturer does not have any recommendations, use common sense and pick color settings that give off less light. For example, experiment with color schemes that provide white characters on a black background. However, do not compromise readability for extra battery life—your eyes are more valuable.

If you run applications that do not allow you to change the color settings, turn the brightness and contrast knobs (if your display has them) to less than their maximum settings.

BATTERY SAVING TIP #2: Use a Disk Cache to Make Your Floppy and Hard Disk Drives Work Less

The primary means of reducing the power drained by drive subsystems is to use them less. One way to make your drives work less is to use a good disk-caching product.

If you use Windows, take advantage of Smartdrive, a disk cache that you load as a device driver in your CONFIG.SYS file. It reduces the amount of times your applications read and write to the drive by caching the most recently used data in RAM. Accessing data in RAM is also much faster. Make sure that you have your Smartdrive device driver loaded and configured correctly.

If you are not using Windows, get a disk cache that is compatible with your laptop system. For example, the cache software provided by Central Point Software's PC Tools can use extended, expanded, or conventional memory. See Chapter 13 for instructions on loading the PC Tools CACHE utility.

Note that cache software will use some of your system's conventional memory, so make sure you have enough RAM to run your applications with a cache product loaded. A cache is most effective if you run it in extended memory, so you should consider purchasing an extra megabyte of extended memory if you do not already have it.

BATTERY SAVING TIP #3: Set Up a RAM Disk for Large Applications

An alternative to using cache software is to set up a RAM disk. RAM disks are pseudo-drives that exist entirely in RAM, enabling faster access to data than is possible with magnetic disks. Keeping copies of applications and data files in a RAM disk is similar to keeping data in a cache, except that you store entire files there, not just the most recently used pieces.

Many applications run entirely from RAM and there is no need to copy them to a RAM drive. However, most larger applications, such as Excel and PageMaker, are *swapped*, meaning that program sections are loaded from disk into RAM as needed. If you use many of a large application's functions, more swapping will occur, and this is when a RAM disk can improve performance.

With DOS applications, you can set up a RAM disk in your CONFIG.SYS file as shown in the example in Figure 12.1. The fourth line in this sample CONFIG.SYS file specifies a 2MB RAM drive that uses extended memory. An example of a corresponding AUTOEXEC.BAT file is shown in Figure 12.2. This sample listing creates a RAM drive labeled D: and a directory called \RAMDIR on that drive. An Excel program file and a read-only spreadsheet (JANBUGET) are then copied from the hard disk to the RAM drive, and the current working directory is set to D:\RAMDIR.

```
FILES = 30
BUFFERS = 30
DEVICE=C:\DOS\HIMEM.SYS
DEVICE=C:\DOS\RAMDRIVE.SYS 2048 512 /E
DEVICE=C:\DOS\ANSI.SYS
```

Figure 12.1: Sample CONFIG.SYS file for a RAM disk

```
ECHO OFF
C:\MOUSE1\MOUSE
PROMPT=$P$G
SET PATH=C:\DOS;C:\WINDOWS;C:\RBFILES;C:\WINWORD;C:\MAC;
SET TEMP=C:\WINDOWS\TEMP
MKDIR D:\RAMDIR
COPY C:\EXCEL\EXCEL.EXE D:\RAMDIR
COPY C:\EXCEL\JANBUGET.XLS D:\RAMDIR
D:
CD D:\RAMDIR
ECHO ON
EXIT
```

Figure 12.2: Sample AUTOEXEC.BAT file for a RAM disk

A major drawback to using a RAM drive is that the data is not periodically written back to your hard disk as it is changed or created. If your laptop's batteries fail while you have a RAM disk in operation, the data currently in the RAM disk is lost (although the original copy of the data is still safe on your hard disk). It is your responsibility to ensure that data is periodically saved back to the hard disk.

Because cache products automatically save your data back to your hard disks, using them is preferable to using a RAM disk. If you want to use a RAM disk, we suggest that you use it only to store copies of your applications or read-only data files that are not edited. Whenever possible, leave data files that will be edited on your hard disk, or you will have to manually copy the data back to disk frequently.

BATTERY SAVING TIP #4:
Use AC Power for Disk-Intensive Work

If possible, save your disk-intensive work for times when you have your laptop plugged into a wall outlet, using AC power. *Disk-intensive* describes any function that requires frequent or prolonged use of disk drives.

For example, it is a bad idea to perform a full backup of your hard disk to floppy disks while running your laptop on battery power. Instead, copy the files that are really necessary to a floppy disk using the DOS COPY command, and do the full backup when you have access to a wall outlet.

Another option is to use your backup utility to copy only one or two directories to a floppy disk. A good utility package, such as PC Tools or The Norton Utilities, provides options that let you make selective backups very quickly, without consuming much power.

Postpone your use of any type of disk-intensive software, such as defragmentation utilities. Using AC power for functions that consume a large percentage of your laptop's power prolongs the life of your batteries.

Backing Up Your Data on the Road

Although laptop computers built by reputable manufacturers are fairly rugged, the amount of abuse they take is still much greater than that suffered by most desktop computers. Laptops are routinely bumped, dropped, spattered by food and drinks, x-rayed, and used in a variety of climates and weather conditions. Because of this, your laptop is more likely (statistically speaking) to fail; and if it does fail, chances are that some of your data will be lost.

All laptop owners should have the capability to back up their data while on the road. The following tips will help you choose the method that best suits your computing habits and budget.

BACKUP STRATEGY TIP #1: Use Floppies, PKZIP, and the DOS COPY Command for Simple Backups

Compressing and then copying your files onto floppy disks is a simple and inexpensive way to back up your files; however, it is efficient only if you do not have a complex directory structure or a large amount of files to back up. If you have ten or fewer directories at the root level and each of these has no more than two or three subdirectories, bring PKZIP (or some other low-cost archiving utility) and a few floppy disks with you. Then you can use the utility to compress and archive the files and directories on your hard disk and copy them to floppy disks using the DOS COPY command. (See Chapter 3 for more information about PKZIP and similar utilities.)

This option works well when you plan to create only a few new documents in two or three different directories. In some cases, such as when you are backing up word processing or spreadsheet files, you will not need PKZIP because your files will fit on a single 720K or 1.44MB floppy disk. But be sure to take an archiving utility if you will be working with larger files, such as those for database or desktop publishing programs.

The primary disadvantage of PKZIP is its low-level user interface. A few bulletin board services, such as CompuServe, provide shareware graphical user interfaces to PKZIP, which improve the utility considerably.

If you don't like the idea of shareware and want a utility with a graphically oriented user interface, use the method described in the following section.

BACKUP STRATEGY TIP #2: Bring Floppy Disks and Professional Backup Software for More Complex Backups

If you have a relatively complex directory structure that consists of more than ten directories at the root level and many subdirectories, PKZIP can get cumbersome. Instead, use a good commercial backup package, such as Central Point Software's Backup program or Fifth Generation Systems' Fastback Plus. These packages are relatively inexpensive (under $100) and easy to use. The Backup program is also provided in Central Point's PC Tools utilities package; see Chapter 13 for instructions on using it.

The major advantage of commercial backup packages is that they perform error detection and correction during backup to ensure that a minor disk error (such as a bad sector) does not render your backup useless. (Error detection is not available with PKZIP or the DOS BACKUP or COPY command.)

A good strategy is to use commercial backup programs in combination with the DOS COPY command and PKZIP. For short trips where you plan to edit only a few files, it is quickest and easiest to simply copy new documents to a floppy disk, and then do a formal backup when you return to your home base of operations. If you are going on a long trip and will be editing many of your files frequently, take a professional backup program with you.

BACKUP STRATEGY TIP #3: Consider an External Hard Drive for Big Backups

If you have large amounts of data to back up during a trip, say more than 20MB, consider purchasing an external hard drive. A variety of these units are available in sizes small enough to fit inside a suitcase.

Most of these external hard drive units attach directly to your computer's parallel port and act as another drive (such as D:). You can back up files directly to the drive without having to insert floppy disks in your laptop as your backup proceeds.

BACKUP STRATEGY TIP #4: Create a Backup before You Leave

Backing up your data on the road is important, but it is equally important to back up your files before you leave. If your system files and applications are damaged while you are on a trip, you have your backups to restore your system to the state it was in before you left.

Simply use your backup software to create an entire compressed version of your hard disk on floppy disks and take them with you. You will also need to take copies of the master disks of your backup software and MS-DOS in order to reinstall your system if necessary.

Information Resources for Traveling Laptop Users

Bulletin board services provide a wealth of information on a wide variety of topics and are an excellent means of tapping into data sources from remote locations. However, there are times when connecting to a bulletin board service is impractical, impossible, too slow, or too expensive. An alternative is to have this information stored directly on your laptop's hard disk.

As laptops increase in power and capacity, taking information resources with you is becoming easier. This new trend in "information to go" is a relatively low-cost means of increasing the value of your laptop.

There are a number of good information systems that any computer user will find helpful. If you travel frequently with your laptop, you may want to investigate the Desktop Flight Guide: North American Edition, a resource offered by Official Airline Guide (OAG).

You can use this database program to identify any direct or connecting flight in North America. You enter the dates of travel, the city you are flying to, your preferred times, and the airlines you would consider using. The program then provides you with a list of all available flights, including the type of aircraft, whether a meal is served, and so on, as shown in the example in Figure 12.3.

Extra Tips for You and Your Laptop 145

```
Itinerary   NotePad   Options   OAGinfo   Help   Quit
                              ═══ Flights ═══
   From: LOS ANGELES, CALIFORNIA (LAX)          Pacific daylight
   To:   NEW YORK NY\NEWARK, NJ (NYC)           Eastern daylight
         ALSO SEE LONG ISLAND MACARTHUR, NY
         AND LONG ISLAND REPUBLIC, NY
   Date: All Dates                  Airline Preferences: None Specified

   Freq     Depart        Arrive        Flight        Class   Equip  Meal Stop
                     CO 1262 Effective 08 Apr
            3:30p  LAX   11:39p  JFK   AA    22     PYBMV     D10    D     0
     x6     3:30p  LAX   11:45p  JFK   MG   600     FCYBM     D8S    D     0
     x6     3:55p  LAX   11:55p  EWR   UA   778     FYBMQ     767    D     0
        ▼   4:00p  LAX   12:04a  JFK   TW     8     FCYBQ     L10    D     0
                    TW    8 BUSINESS CLASS   AVBL
            9:50p  LAX    5:47a  EWR   UA   138     FnYnBMQ   D8S    S     0
           10:00p  LAX    6:04a  JFK   PA   100     FCYBM     747    S     0
           10:00p  LAX    6:10a  JFK   AA    10     FnYnBMV   D10    S     0

  F1=Help  F4=NotePad  F9=Connections   ↑↓=Move  ↵=Details  Esc=Close
           OAG FlightDisk (TM)             |     Effective Apr 7-30, 1991
```

Figure 12.3: OAG Flight Guide screen

The OAG Travel Service is subscription-oriented; you receive monthly updates of the database for a yearly fee.

If you have a modem, you may also be interested in the OAG Electronic Edition Travel Service. Three of the databases in this extensive bulletin board system may be extremely useful to you while on the road:

- Major Airport Updates: This database, which is updated every 10 minutes, provides arrival, departure, and gate assignments for 17 major airports in the United States.

- Worldwide Weather from AccuWeather: This database gives detailed weather predictions and current conditions on a city-by-city basis.

- Nationwide Intelligence: This database provides basic information specific to most airports in the United States. Telephone numbers and locations for each airline, rental car company, and other business resources are listed.

You can use the Desktop Flight Guide in conjunction with OAG's electronic booking program (available through the Electronic Edition Travel Service) to review your flight options off-line and then book the flight with your laptop and modem.

For the OAG Electronic Edition Travel Service, there is a one-time setup fee and per minute connection charge for on-line services.

If you are interested in OAG information resources, contact:

Official Airline Guides
2000 Clearwater Drive
Oak Brook, IL 60521
(800) 323-3537 or (312) 574-6096

THIRTEEN

Quick Guide to Application Commands

148 The Laptop User's Survival Guide

This chapter contains commonly used commands for ten popular programs:

- MS-DOS (version 3.3 or later)
- Windows 3.0
- WordPerfect 5.1
- MS Word 5.5
- Lotus 1-2-3
- Excel for Windows
- dBASE III
- PageMaker for Windows
- Crosstalk for Windows
- PC Tools 5.5 and 6.0

Although you might not have any of the programs listed here, it is likely that you will encounter them while traveling with your laptop. Use this reference guide to accomplish basic tasks with these applications.

In the keyboard command sequences included in the listings, a keystroke sequence such as Shift-Tab or Ctrl-B means hold down the first key in the sequence while pressing the second key. The exception to this rule is the Alt key—you do not have to hold it down while you press the next key in the sequence. Additionally, the term *arrow key* refers to one of the four arrow keys on the keyboard (up, down, left, or right).

Commonly Used MS-DOS Commands

The following listing includes many commonly used MS-DOS commands and examples of their functions.

Quick Guide to Application Commands

APPEND: Displays the current search path for data files.

APPEND B:\MEMOS; D:\FORMS

Makes DOS search the two given directories, MEMOS on drive B: and FORMS on drive D:, for data files.

ASSIGN: See the SUBST command.

ATTRIB: Sets or displays file attributes.

ATTRIB *.*

Displays the attributes of all files in a directory.

ATTRIB +R File.DAT

Sets the read-only attribute of File.DAT.

ATTRIB +A File.DAT

Sets the archive attribute of File.DAT.

ATTRIB −R *.*

Turns off read-only mode for all files in current directory.

ATTRIB +R A:\USER /S

Sets all files and subdirectories in A:\USER to read-only.

ATTRIB +H Secret.BAT

Sets the file Secret.BAT as a hidden file (it will not appear in a directory listing).

BACKUP: Backs up a group of files to a specified disk.

BACKUP C:\USER\SAM A:

Backs up all files in the \USER\SAM directory to drive A:.

BACKUP C:\CHARLIE\FILES*.DOC A: /S

> Backs up all files with the .DOC extension in the \CHARLIE\FILES directory on drive C: to the disk in drive A:. The /S switch specifies that all files in all subdirectories in \CHARLIE\FILES are to be backed up as well.

BREAK: Makes Ctrl-C interrupt disk reads and writes.

BREAK ON

> Extends Ctrl-C to interrupting disk reads and writes.

BREAK OFF

> Makes MS-DOS respond to Ctrl-C only during screen, keyboard, and printer reads and writes.

CD: Changes from the current directory to the specified directory.

CD

> Displays current working directory.

CD \USER\LETTERS

> Changes to the \USER\LETTERS directory.

CD TEMP

> Changes to the TEMP subdirectory of the current directory.

CHCP: Displays or changes the current code page.

CHCP 437

> Sets the code page to the default code page for the United States.

CHCP 850

> Sets the code page for multilingual capability.

Quick Guide to Application Commands 151

CHKDSK: Provides information on the status of the specified disk drive and optionally fixes any errors it encounters.

>CHKDSK
>
>>Provides information on the status of the default disk drive.
>
>CHKDSK C:
>
>>Provides the disk status for drive C:.
>
>CHKDSK A: /F
>
>>Checks the disk in drive A: for any errors and fixes the ones it finds if it can.
>
>CHKDSK B: /V
>
>>Displays each file's name as the disk is scanned.

CLS: Clears the screen.

COMP: Compares the contents of two sets of files and displays the results on the screen.

>COMP File1.TXT File2.TXT
>
>>Compares the contents of the files File1.TXT and File2.TXT.

COPY: Copies one or more files from one location to another.

>COPY A.TXT B.TXT
>
>>Makes a copy of the file A.TXT and names it B.TXT.
>
>COPY B:*.*
>
>>Copies all files in drive B: to the current directory.
>
>COPY Myfile.DOC \LETTERS\PRIVATE
>
>>Copies Myfile.DOC to the directory \LETTERS\PRIVATE.

COPY *.ASC Myfiles.ALL

> Combines all files with the extension .ASC into a single file named Myfiles.ALL.

COPY A.TXT + B.TXT + C.TXT   All.TXT

> Appends the files B.TXT and C.TXT to the file A.TXT and names the result All.TXT.

DATE: Displays and sets the system date.

DATE

> Displays currently selected date.

DATE 03-24-92

> Sets the date to March 24, 1992.

DEL: Deletes one or more specified files.

DEL Report.DOC

> Deletes the file Report.DOC.

DEL *.DOC

> Deletes all files with the extension .DOC in the current directory.

DEL /P *.DOC

> Same as DEL *.DOC, but DOS asks you to confirm each deletion.

DIR: Displays a listing of files.

DIR

> Lists all files in the current working directory.

DIR A:*.TMP

> Lists all files on the disk in drive A: with the extension .TMP.

Quick Guide to Application Commands

DIR /P

> Lists all files in the current directory and prevents the list from scrolling off the screen.

DIR /W \MASM\BIN

> Lists all files in the directory \MASM\BIN in wide format.

DISKCOMP: Compares two diskettes and reports any differences.

DISKCOMP A: B:

> Compares the contents of the disk in drive A: to the contents of the disk in drive B:.

DISKCOPY: Copies the contents of one floppy disk to another (not from a floppy disk to a hard disk).

DISKCOPY A: B:

> Copies the contents of the floppy disk in drive A: to the floppy disk in drive B:.

EDIT (MS-DOS 5.0): Starts the MS-DOS EDIT full-screen file editor.

EDIT

> Starts the editor.

EDIT Myfile.ABC

> Starts the EDIT program and loads the file Myfile.ABC.

EDLIN: Starts EDLIN, the line-oriented MS-DOS editor. In EDLIN, enter ? to display a list of EDLIN commands. At the * prompt, type the line number to go to a specific line in the text; type l to display all lines in a file. To replace a line, type the line number you want to replace, and then type your new text. (Press Return to end the line.) To insert a line of text in a file, type **I,** and then type the line. To turn off insert mode, press Return, then Ctrl-C.

EXIT: Exits the current command program (if you have multiple DOS sessions running concurrently).

FASTOPEN: Decreases the amount of time necessary to open frequently used files or directories.

>FASTOPEN C:=50

>>Stores the location of up to 50 files on drive C: in a special cache so it can find them quickly. Uses some extra RAM.

FC: Compares two files or two sets of files.

>FC /A June.TXT July.TXT

>>Compares the contents of the two text files June.TXT and July.TXT.

>FC /A /C June.TXT July.TXT

>>Same as previous example, but ignores case.

>FC /A /N Micro.TXT Macro.TXT

>>Compares the two files Micro.TXT and Macro.TXT, displaying line numbers.

FDISK: Partitions a hard disk (does not work with drives used in SUBST or JOIN commands).

FIND: Searches for a string of text in a file or files.

>FIND "Curie's theory" Science.TXT

>>Finds the string *Curie's theory* in the file Science.TXT.

>FIND /C "mix & match" File.DAT

>>Reports the number of lines in the file File.DAT that contain the string *mix & match*.

TREE /C: | FIND ".DOC"

    Lists all the files with .DOC extensions in drive C:.

FORMAT: Formats a floppy or hard disk.

    FORMAT A: /F:1.44

        Formats a 1.44MB floppy disk in drive A:.

    FORMAT A: /F:720

        Formats a 720K floppy disk in drive A:.

    FORMAT A: /S

        Formats the floppy disk in drive A: and copies the operating system to it.

HELP (MS-DOS 5.0): Provides limited help on DOS commands.

    HELP COPY

        Provides help on the MS-DOS COPY command.

    HELP FORMAT

        Provides help on the MS-DOS FORMAT command.

JOIN: Joins a disk drive to a directory path join.

    JOIN G: C:\LETTERS

        Associates drive G: with the directory C:\LETTERS.

    JOIN G: /D

        Reverses the join performed on drive G:.

LABEL: Changes a disk's volume label.

    LABEL B:Reports

        Labels the floppy disk in drive B: as *Reports*.

MD: Makes a new directory.

> MD NEWDIR
>
>> Makes a new directory called NEWDIR in the current working directory.
>
> MD B:\TEST\PROGRAMS
>
>> Makes a new directory called PROGRAMS in the \TEST directory on drive B:.

MEM: Lists the amount of memory in use, free memory, expanded memory usage, and extended memory usage.

> MEM /PROGRAM
>
>> Lists memory usage for all currently running programs.

MIRROR (MS-DOS 5.0): Stores the file allocation table (FAT) of the specified disk (used for data recovery).

> MIRROR C:
>
>> Stores the FAT of disk C: in a file.
>
> MIRROR C: /TC
>
>> Stores the FAT of disk C: and installs the deletion-tracking TSR program.
>
> MIRROR /U
>
>> Unloads the deletion-tracking TSR from memory.

MODE: Displays or changes the status of various communications, printer, and video ports.

> MODE COM1:
>
>> Displays the status of the COM1 port and returns an error if it is not operational.

Quick Guide to Application Commands

MODE LPT1: 80,8

>Sets the parallel printer port to support 80 columns at 8 lines per inch.

MODE 40, 25

>Puts the screen in large character mode (works only with ANSI.SYS).

MODE 80,50

>Puts the screen in small character mode (works only with ANSI.SYS).

MODE COM1:9600 ODD 8

>Sets the COM1 port to 9600 baud, odd parity, and 8 data bits.

MORE: Suppresses scrolling of information off the screen.

TYPE Myfile.TXT ¦ MORE

>Displays the file Myfile.TXT on your screen one page at a time.

MORE < Invoice.DAT

>Displays the file Invoice.DAT one screen at a time.

PATH: Displays and specifies the path.

PATH

>Displays the currently set path.

PATH;

>Deletes the current path and sets it to no path.

PATH C:\PROGS; \DOS\COMMANDS

>Tells DOS to search for commands first in \PROGS, then in \DOS\COMMANDS.

PRINT: Prints a text file.

PRINT /D:LPT1

Sets the print device name to LPT1 (parallel port 1).

PRINT /D:COM1

Sets the print device name to COM1 (serial port number 1).

PRINT Catalog.TXT

Prints the file Catalog.TXT to the printer set in the PRINT/D: DEVICE command.

PRINT /T

Removes all print jobs from the print queue.

PROMPT: Changes the DOS prompt.

PROMPT $G

Sets the prompt equal to the > character.

PROMPT $P

Sets the prompt to the current directory.

PROMPT GP

Sets the prompt to > followed by the current directory.

PROMPT TP

Sets the prompt to the current time followed by the current directory.

RECOVER: Recovers information from a corrupted file or drive.

RECOVER Noluck.BAD

Recovers any good sectors from the file Noluck.BAD.

RECOVER B:

Recovers all files on the disk in drive B:.

Quick Guide to Application Commands

REN: Changes the name of a file.

    REN Graphics.EXE Graphics.COM

        Renames the file Graphics.EXE to Graphics.COM.

    REN *.DOC *.OLD

        Changes the extension of all .DOC files to .OLD.

REPLACE: Replaces files with newer versions.

    REPLACE A:*.DOC C:\PRESS*.DOC /U

        Replaces files with .DOC extensions in C:\PRESS with newer files on drive A:.

    REPLACE A:*.DOC C:\PRESS*.DOC /U /R

        Same as previous example, but overwrites read-only files.

    REPLACE *.TXT B:*.DOC /S

        Replaces .DOC files on drive B: with *.TXT files. Searches subdirectories on drive B:.

RESTORE: Restores files that were backed up with the BACKUP command.

    RESTORE A: C:\WALTER\SAVE

        Restores the files on the disk in drive A: to the directory \WALTER\SAVE on the disk in drive C:.

RD: Deletes an empty directory.

    RD \USER\JEFF

        Deletes the subdirectory JEFF from the directory USER.

SELECT: Installs MS-DOS on a hard disk or floppy disk.

SELECT MENU

　Allows you to change your existing MS-DOS settings and creates AUTOEXEC.BAT and CONFIG.SYS files.

SET: Sets two strings equal to each other in the environment space.

　SET info = C:\WORDS\RUN\Readme.TXT

　　Sets the string *info* to the file C:\WORDS\RUN\Readme.TXT.

SETVER (MS-DOS 5.0): Displays a list of the current versions reported to different programs.

　SETVER Prog.EXE 4.01

　　Forces MS-DOS to report version number 4.01 to Prog.EXE.

SORT: Sorts data in a file by alphabetical order.

　SORT < Clients.TXT

　　Sorts the file Clients.TXT alphabetically by the first character of each line.

　DIR ¦ SORT /+14

　　Sorts a directory listing by file size (the file size designation begins in the fourteenth position of the directory listing).

　DIR ¦ SORT /+14 ¦ MORE

　　Same as previous example, but prevents output from scrolling off the screen.

SUBST: Substitutes a drive letter for a path name.

　SUBST G: A:\LETTERS\CLIENTS\FORMS

　　Assigns the drive G: to the path A:\LETTERS\CLIENTS\FORMS.

　SUBST G: /D

　　Reverses the substitution in the previous example.

Quick Guide to Application Commands

SYS: Copies MS-DOS system files, including all hidden files, to another drive.

SYS A

Copies MS-DOS system files from the current drive to drive A:.

TIME: Displays and sets the system time.

TIME

Displays the currently selected time.

TIME 14:02:23

Resets the system clock to 2:02 PM plus 23 seconds.

TREE: Displays all the directories and their subdirectories graphically.

TREE

Displays a graphic representation of the directories and subdirectories on the hard disk.

TREE /F

Displays the names of the files in each subdirectory.

TYPE: Displays a text file on the screen.

TYPE Textfile.TXT

Displays the contents of the file Textfile.TXT on your screen.

TYPE Textfile.TXT | MORE

Same as previous example, but prevents data from scrolling off the screen.

UNDELETE (MS-DOS 5.0): Recovers a file that has been deleted by the DEL command.

UNDELETE Datafil.DOC

Recovers the file Datafil.DOC that was just deleted.

UNDELETE /LIST

> Displays a list of all the files in the directory that are available for undeletion.

UNDELETE *.TXT /ALL

> Recovers all files with the extension .TXT and does not prompt you for confirmation.

UNFORMAT (MS-DOS 5.0): Restores a disk that has been erased by the MS-DOS FORMAT command.

UNFORMAT C:

> Unformats the disk in drive C:.

UNFORMAT C: /J

> Verifies that the file created by the MIRROR command has been saved.

UNFORMAT C: /U

> Performs an unformat, but does not use the file created by the MIRROR command.

VER: Indicates which version of MS-DOS you are running on your computer.

VOL: Displays a disk volume label.

VOL B:

> Displays the label of the disk in drive B:.

XCOPY: Copies files and directories, including subdirectories.

XCOPY A: B: /S /E

> Copies all directories and subdirectories from drive A: to drive B:.

XCOPY A: B: /D:04-06-1991

Copies all root-level directories dated after April 6, 1991, on drive A: to drive B:.

Windows Quick Keys

You may not be able to use your mouse with Windows because you do not have enough room, you forgot to bring it, or it is not operating properly. Even if you can use your mouse, you may prefer to use the Windows quick keys, which are shown in the following listings.

Windows Program Manager Menu Key Sequences

Key Sequence	Function
File Menu	
Alt-F N	Creates a new program item or group
Alt-F O	Runs the currently selected program or opens the currently selected document
Alt-F M	Moves a program item from its current group to a new group
Alt-F C	Copies a program item from its current group to a new group
Alt-F D	Deletes a program item
Alt-F P	Changes the properties of a program item
Alt-F R	Runs a program (type in its DOS path name)
Alt-F X	Exits Windows

Key Sequence	Function
Options Menu	
Alt-O N	Selects the Auto Arrange feature
Alt-O M	Selects the Minimize on Use feature
Window Menu	
Alt-W C or Shift-F5	Cascades Program Manager windows
Alt-W T or Shift-F4	Tiles Program Manager windows
Alt-W *number*	Selects the window designated in the Window menu by *number*
Help Menu	
Alt-H I	Gets an index of help topics
Alt-H K	Gets information about keyboard command sequences
Alt-H B	Gets help on basic Windows skills
Alt-H C	Gets help on Windows commands
Alt-H P	Gets help on Windows procedures
Alt-H G	Opens a glossary of Windows terms
Alt-H U	Provides information about using help
Alt-H A	Provides information about the Program Manager
General	
Alt-right arrow	Moves from the currently selected main menu item to the next item
Alt-left arrow	Moves from the currently selected main menu item to the previous item
Down arrow	Moves down one menu item in a currently open menu.

Quick Guide to Application Commands

Key Sequence	Function
Up arrow	Moves up one menu item in a currently open menu
Alt-down arrow	Opens a menu
Ctrl-Tab	Moves among group windows and icons

General Windows System Functions

Key Sequence	Function
Ctrl-Esc	Allows you to switch from one running task to another through a dialog box list
Alt-Esc	Switches to the next application window but does not restore minimized icons
Alt-Tab	Switches to the next running task, restoring any minimized icons
PrtScreen	Captures the current screen image and copies it to the clipboard
Alt-PrtScreen	Captures the currently selected window image and copies it to the clipboard
Arrow keys	Move among items in an active group window; also lets you move or resize individual windows after selecting Ctrl-F7 (move a window) or Ctrl-F8 (resize a window)

Manipulating Application Windows

Key Sequence	Function
Alt-spacebar	Opens the Control menu for an application window
Alt-hyphen	Opens the Control menu for a document window
Alt-spacebar R	Restores the currently active window

Key Sequence	Function
Alt-spacebar N	Minimizes the currently active window to an icon
Alt-spacebar M	Moves the currently active window
Alt-spacebar S	Resizes the currently active window
Alt-spacebar X	Maximizes a window
Alt-F4	Closes the currently active application window
Alt-Return	Toggles a non-Windows application from a window to full screen and back

Working with Dialog Boxes

Key Sequence	Function
Tab	Moves forward from one major item to the next major item
Shift-Tab	Moves backward from one major item to the previous major item
Right arrow	Moves to the right one item in a list of items
Left arrow	Moves to the left one item in a list of items
Up arrow	Moves up one item in a list of items
Down arrow	Moves down one item in a list of items
Home	Moves to the beginning of a block of text in a text box
End	Moves to the end of a block of text in a text box
Shift-Home	Deselects any selected text in a text box
Shift-End	Extends any selected text to the end of the line of text
Spacebar	Toggles a check box or selection in a list on and off

Quick Guide to Application Commands

Key Sequence	Function
Return	"Presses" the currently highlighted button
Shift-right arrow	Highlights the next character in a text field
Shift-left arrow	Highlights the previous character in a text field
Esc	Removes the dialog box without saving any changes you made to it
Ctrl-/	Selects all items in a list box
Ctrl-\	Deselects all items in a list box except the current selection

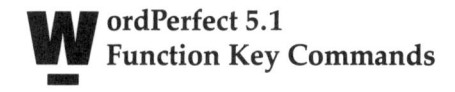

WordPerfect 5.1 Function Key Commands

For easy reference, the WordPerfect function key commands are listed first by function name, and then by key sequence.

WordPerfect 5.1 Commands by Function

Function	Key Sequence
Block	Alt-F4
Bold	F6
Cancel	F1
Center	Shift-F6
Columns/Tables	Alt-F7
Date/Outline	Shift-F5
End Field	F9
Exit	F7

The Laptop User's Survival Guide

Function	Key Sequence
Flush Right	Alt-F6
Font	Ctrl-F8
Footnote	Ctrl-F7
Format	Shift-F8
Graphics	Alt-F9
Help	F3
Indent Left	F4
Indent Right	Shift-F4
List	F5
Macro	Alt-F10
Macro Define	Ctrl-F10
Mark Text	Alt-F5
Merge Codes	Shift-F9
Merge/Sort	Ctrl-F9
Move	Ctrl-F4
Print	Shift-F7
Replace	Alt-F2
Retrieve	Shift-F10
Reveal Codes	Alt-F3
Save	F10
Screen	Ctrl-F3
Search	F2
Search/Replace	Shift-F2
Setup	Shift-F1

Quick Guide to Application Commands

Function	Key Sequence
Shell	Ctrl-F1
Spell	Ctrl-F2
Style	Alt-F8
Switch	Shift-F3
Tab Align	Ctrl-F6
Text In/Out	Ctrl-F5
Thesaurus	Alt-F1
Underline	F8

WordPerfect 5.1 Commands by Key Sequence

Key Sequence	Function
F1	Cancel
Shift-F1	Setup
Ctrl-F1	Shell
Alt-F1	Thesaurus
F2	Search
Shift-F2	Search/Replace
Ctrl-F2	Spell
Alt-F2	Replace
F3	Help
Shift-F3	Switch
Ctrl-F3	Screen
Alt-F3	Reveal Codes
F4	Indent Left

Key Sequence	Function
Shift-F4	Indent Right
Ctrl-F4	Move
Alt-F4	Block
F5	List
Shift-F5	Date/Outline
Ctrl-F5	Text In/Out
Alt-F5	Mark Text
F6	Bold
Shift-F6	Center
Ctrl-F6	Tab Align
Alt-F6	Flush Right
F7	Exit
Shift-F7	Print
Ctrl-F7	Footnote
Alt-F7	Columns/Tables
F8	Underline
Shift-F8	Format
Ctrl-F8	Font
Alt-F8	Style
F9	End Field
Shift-F9	Merge Codes
Ctrl-F9	Merge/Sort
Alt-F9	Graphics
F10	Save

Quick Guide to Application Commands 171

Key Sequence	Function
Shift-F10	Retrieve
Ctrl-F10	Macro Define
Alt-F10	Macro

MS Word 5.5 Function Key Commands

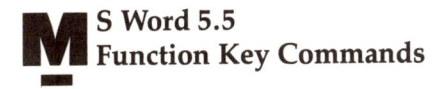

The following sections list MS Word 5.5 function key commands by function, and then by key sequence.

MS Word 5.5 Commands by Function

Function	Key Sequence
Activate Menu Bar	F10
Activate Ruler	Shift-Ctrl-F10
Adjust Size of Active Window	Ctrl-F8
Calculate	F2
Case Selection	Shift-F3
Display Mode	Alt-F9
Edit Copy	Alt-F3
Edit Go To	F5
Edit Repeat	F4
Exit	Alt-F4
Expand Glossary	F3
File Open	Alt-Ctrl-F2
File Print	Alt-Shift-Ctrl-F2

Function	Key Sequence
File Save As (active)	Alt-Shift-F2
File Save As (current)	Alt-F2
Format Character	Ctrl-F2
Help	F1
Insert Bookmark	Shift-Ctrl-F5
Macro Record	Ctrl-F3
Maximize Window	Ctrl-F10
Move to Active Window	Ctrl-F7
Move to Next Field	F11
Move to Next Window	Ctrl-F6
Move to Next Window in Active Pane	F6
Move to Previous Field	Shift-F11
Move to Previous Window	Shift-Ctrl-F6
Move to Previous Window in Active Pane	Shift-F6
Next Field	Alt-F1
Outline Edit/Organize	Shift-F5
Outline Mode (on/off)	Shift-F5
Overtype Mode (on/off)	Alt-F5
Preview Document	Ctrl-F9
Previous Field	Alt-Shift-F1
Print Active Document	Shift-F9
Search Repeat	Shift-F10
Select	F8
Select Column (on/off)	Shift-Ctrl-F8

Quick Guide to Application Commands

Function	Key Sequence
Select Entire Document	Shift-F10
Select Paragraph	Alt-F10
Select Sentence	Alt-F8
Select Shrink	Shift-F8
Select Word or Next Word	Alt-F6
Show Line Breaks (on/off)	Alt-F7
Spell Checking	F7
Thesaurus	Shift-F7
Update Link	F9
Window Close	Ctrl-F4
Window Restore	Ctrl-F5

MS Word 5.5 Commands by Key Sequence

Key Sequence	Function
F1	Help
Alt-F1	Next Field
Alt-Shift-F1	Previous Field
F2	Calculate
Shift-F2	Outline Mode (on/off)
Ctrl-F2	Format Character
Alt-F2	File Save As (Current)
Alt-Ctrl-F2	File Open
Alt-Shift-Ctrl-F2	File Print
F3	Expand Glossary

174 The Laptop User's Survival Guide

Key Sequence	Function
Shift-F3	Case Selection
Ctrl-F3	Macro Record
Alt-F3	Edit Copy
F4	Edit Repeat
Shift-F4	Search Repeat
Ctrl-F4	Window Close
Alt-F4	Exit
F5	Edit Go To
Shift-F5	Outline Edit/Organize
Ctrl-F5	Window Restore
Alt-F5	Overtype Mode (on/off)
Shift-Ctrl-F5	Insert Bookmark
F6	Move to Previous Window in Active Pane
Ctrl-F6	Move to Next Window
Alt-F6	Select Word or Next Word
Shift-Ctrl-F6	Move to Previous Window
F7	Spell Checking
Shift-F7	Thesaurus
Ctrl-F7	Move to Active Window
Alt-F7	Show Line Breaks (on/off)
F8	Select
Shift-F8	Select Shrink
Ctrl-F8	Adjust Size of Active Window
Alt-F8	Select Sentence

Quick Guide to Application Commands 175

Key Sequence	Function
Shift-Ctrl-F8	Select Column (on/off)
F9	Update Link
Shift-F9	Print Active Document
Ctrl-F9	Preview Document
Alt-F9	Display Mode
F10	Activate Menu Bar
Shift-F10	Select Entire Document
Ctrl-F10	Maximize Window
Alt-F10	Select Paragraph
Shift-Ctrl-F10	Activate Ruler
F11	Move to Next Field
Shift-F11	Move to Previous Field

Twenty-Five Lotus 1-2-3 Commands

The following are 25 basic keystroke commands that will help you navigate through Lotus 1-2-3 and its menu system.

Command	Function
/Copy	Copies numbers, labels, formulas, or a range of cells to new cells on the spreadsheet
/Data Sort	Reorders rows within a range based on the value of the sort key
/File Dir	Selects the current directory that 1-2-3 is using to store files

Command	Function
/File Erase	Removes one or more files
/File New	Creates a blank new worksheet
/File Open	Loads an existing 1-2-3 file and keeps other files open (version 3.1 only)
/File Retrieve	Loads an existing 1-2-3 file
/File Save	Saves the current 1-2-3 worksheet file
/Print Cancel	Cancels all print jobs
/Print File	Prints information to a file instead of a printer
/Print Printer	Prints information from a worksheet to your printer
/Print Printer Align	Sets the line counter to zero and the page number to one
/Print Printer Clear	Clears special print settings and returns settings to their defaults
/Print Printer Go	Begins transmitting the print range to the printer
/Print Printer Range	Determines how much of the worksheet is printed
/Print Printer Quit	Leaves the Printer menu
/Print Quit	Leaves the Print menu
/Quit	Exits 1-2-3
/Range Erase	Deletes entries in worksheet cells
/Range Format	Determines how numbers appear on the worksheet

Quick Guide to Application Commands 177

Command	Function
/Range Search	Performs a search-and-replace operation on the selected range
/Worksheet Column	Controls the characteristics of a column
/Worksheet Delete	Deletes a column, row, or worksheet
/Worksheet Erase	Erases the active file from memory
/Worksheet Global Default Dir	Sets a directory as the default directory for file management

Excel for Windows Keystrokes and Commands

The following sections list many of the keystrokes for working with Excel for Windows. They are grouped as follows:

- Worksheet cursor movement
- Worksheet item selection
- Formula bar keystrokes
- Function key and Ctrl key shortcuts
- Worksheet cell formatting shortcuts
- Codes for formatting worksheet headers and footers (set through the Page Setup option on the File menu)

Excel Worksheet Cursor-Movement Keystrokes

Key Sequence	Function
Arrow keys	Move one cell in the direction of the arrow
Home	Moves to the beginning of the current row

Key Sequence	Function
End	Moves to the end of the current row
Page Down	Moves down the length of one window
Page Up	Moves up the length of one window
Ctrl-End	Moves to the end of the worksheet
Ctrl-arrow key	Moves one block of data in the direction of the arrow
Ctrl-Home	Moves to start of the worksheet
Ctrl-Page Up	Moves left the length of one window
Ctrl-Page Down	Moves right the length of one window

Excel Worksheet Selection Keystrokes

Key Sequence	Function
Shift-arrow key	Extends selection one cell in the direction of the arrow
Shift-Home	Extends selection to the beginning of the row
Shift-End	Extends selection to the end of the row
Ctrl-Shift-Home	Extends selection to the beginning of the worksheet
Ctrl-Shift-End	Extends selection to the end of the worksheet
Ctrl-Shift-arrow key	Extends selection one block in the direction of the arrow
Shift-arrow key	Extends selection one cell in the direction of the arrow
Shift-Page Up	Extends selection up the length of a window

Quick Guide to Application Commands

Key Sequence	Function
Shift-Page Down	Extends selection down the length of a window
Ctrl-Shift-spacebar	Selects the entire worksheet
Ctrl-Shift-Page Up	Extends selection left the length of a window
Ctrl-Shift-Page Down	Extends selection right the length of a window

Excel Formula Bar Keystrokes

Key Sequence	Function
F2	Activates the formula bar for editing
Home	Moves to the beginning of the line
End	Moves to the end of the line
Ctrl-End	Moves to the end of the formula bar
Arrow key	Moves one character in the direction of the arrow
Ctrl-arrow key	Moves one word in the direction of the arrow
Delete	Deletes the character to the right of the cursor
Shift-Delete	Cuts the selected text to the clipboard
Backspace	Deletes the character to the left of the cursor
Shift-Insert	Pastes text from the clipboard
Ctrl-Insert	Copies the selected text to the clipboard
Ctrl-;	Inserts the current date into the formula bar
Ctrl-:	Inserts the current time into the formula bar

Excel Function Key and Ctrl Key Shortcuts

Key Sequence	Function
Ctrl-=	Calculate Now
F1	Help
Shift-F1	Context-Sensitive Help
Alt-F1	Create New Chart (of the selected data)
Alt-Shift-F1	Create New Worksheet
Alt-Ctrl-F1	Create New Macro Sheet
F2	Activate Formula Bar
Shift-F2	Formula Note
Ctrl-F2	Window Show Info
Alt-F2	File Save As
Alt-Shift-F2	File Save
Alt-Ctrl-F2	File Open
F3	Formula Paste Name
Shift-F3	Formula Paste Function
Ctrl-F3	Formula Define Name
Ctrl-Shift-F3	Formula Create Names
F4	Formula Reference
Ctrl-F4	Close Current Document Window
Alt-F4	Exit Excel
F5	Formula Goto
Shift-F5	Formula Find
Ctrl-F5	Restore Active Document Window

Quick Guide to Application Commands

Key Sequence	Function
Alt-F5	Restore Application Window
F6	Next Pane
Shift-F6	Previous Pane
Ctrl-F6	Next Document Window
Ctrl-Shift-F6	Previous Document Window
F7	Formula Find
Shift-F7	Formula Find (previous cell)
Ctrl-F7	Control Move (document window)
Alt-F7	Control Move (application window)
F8	Extend (on/off)
Shift-F8	Add
Ctrl-F8	Control Size (document window)
Alt-F8	Control Size (application window)
F9	Options Calculate Now
Shift-F9	Options Calculate Document
Alt-F9	Control Minimize (application window)
F10	Activate Menu Bar
Ctrl-F10	Control Maximize (document window)
Alt-F10	Control Maximize (application window)

Excel Cell Formatting Keystrokes

Key Sequence	Format of Selected Cells
Ctrl-~	General format
Ctrl-!	0.00 format

Key Sequence	Format of Selected Cells
Ctrl-#	d-mmm-yy format
Ctrl-@	h:mm AM/PM format
Ctrl-%	0% format
Ctrl-1	Font 1
Ctrl-2	Font 2
Ctrl-3	Font 3
Ctrl-4	Font 4

Excel Page Setup Dialog Box Header and Footer Codes

Characters	Function
&L	Aligns following characters to the left
&R	Aligns following characters to the right
&C	Centers following characters
&B	Prints the header or footer in bold
&I	Prints the header or footer in italic
&D	Prints the date
&T	Prints the time
&F	Prints the name of the document
&P	Prints the page number
&P + n	Prints the page number plus n
&P − n	Prints the page number minus n

Quick Guide to Application Commands

dBASE III
Commands and Keystrokes

The following dBASE III reference listing includes 25 commonly used navigational commands given from the dBASE dot prompt (a period on the left side of the screen) and examples of their use. These commands are followed by a list of basic keystroke commands.

ASSIST

Accesses menu-driven aid for using dBASE.

BROWSE

Displays up to 17 rows of records.

BROWSE FIELDS

Displays the contents of the fields by the specified parameter.

BROWSE FIELDS lastname, firstname

Displays fields by last and first name.

COPY FILE

Duplicates any file (similar to the MS-DOS COPY command).

COPY FILE Myfile.TXT TO Newfile.TXT

Copies the file Myfile.TXT to the file named Newfile.TXT.

COPY STRUCTURE TO

Duplicates the structure of the current database file in use (see USE command) to a new, empty database file.

COPY STRUCTURE TO Newfile

Copies the empty database structure of the current file to the new database file Newfile.DBF.

CREATE

    Creates a new database file structure.

  CREATE Myfile

    Creates a new database file named Myfile.DBF.

CREATE REPORT

    Creates a report form file.

  CREATE REPORT Myfile1

    Starts the creation of a report for the database file Myfile1.

DELETE

    Marks a record for deletion. The PACK command will then permanently remove any records that have been marked for deletion.

  DELETE FOR lastname = "Smith"

    Marks for deletion any record that has the last name of Smith.

DIR

    Lists the names of database files.

DISPLAY STATUS

    Lists current information about the active databases.

DO

    Starts a program or procedure.

  DO Menu

    Starts the program Menu.PRG.

Quick Guide to Application Commands

EJECT

    Sends a form-feed command to the printer.

GOTO

    Positions the record pointer on a specific record in the database file.

    GOTO TOP

        Goes to the first record in the database file.

    GOTO BOTTOM

        Goes to the last record of the file.

    GOTO 24

        Goes to record number 24 in the file.

INDEX ON

    Creates an index file for the current database to facilitate sorting based on a key field.

    INDEX ON lastname TO Index1

        Creates an index file named Index1.NDX.

LIST

    Lists database records and fields.

    LIST lastname, firstname

        Lists the contents of the last name and first name fields for all records in the database.

    LIST lastname, firstname TO PRINT

        Lists the contents of the last name and first name fields for all records in the database and sends the result to the printer.

LIST lastname, firstname TO PRINT FOR city = "Peoria"

Lists the contents of the last name and first name fields for any record that has Peoria as its city and sends the result to the printer.

LIST STRUCTURE

Displays the name, width, and type of all fields defined in the current database file.

LOCATE

Finds the first record that meets the specified condition.

LOCATE FOR lastname = "Smith"

Finds the first record that has the last name Smith.

MODIFY

Alters an existing file or report.

MODIFY REPORT Myfile1

Opens the report Myfile1 for editing.

MODIFY STRUCTURE Myfile

Opens the file Myfile for editing the database structure.

PACK

Removes records marked for deletion (see DELETE command).

QUIT

Closes all files and exits dBASE.

REINDEX

Rebuilds active index files. (Use this command when the key field of any record has been modified.)

Quick Guide to Application Commands

REINDEX Index1

Rebuilds the index file Index1.

REPORT FORM

Opens a report form file.

REPORT FORM Myfile1

Starts the report Myfile1 for the database file Myfile.

REPORT FORM Myfile1 TO PRINT

Starts the report Myfile1 for the database file Myfile and sends it to the printer.

SEEK

Locates the first record with an index key matching the expression.

SEEK "Smith"

Looks for a record that contains the last name Smith.

SET

Establishes control over a number of dBASE parameters.

USE

Opens a database file to be used until another database is opened with the USE command.

USE Myfile

Opens a database file named Myfile.

ZAP

Removes all records from the current database file.

dBASE Keystroke Commands

Key Sequence	Function
Page Down	Moves to the next screen (or record)
Page Up	Moves to the previous screen (or record)
Ctrl-Page Up	Enters the Memo field editor (while the cursor is in the Memo field)
Ctrl-Home	Saves the current Memo field and exits the editor
Ctrl-U	Marks a record for deletion
Ctrl-N	Inserts a new line or field
Ctrl-W	Saves changes and exits
Ctrl-Q	Exits without saving changes

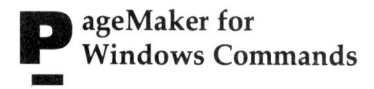

PageMaker for Windows Commands

The following are basic PageMaker for Windows commands. The list includes the function, menu option, and keystrokes for each command.

Function	Menu Option	Key Sequence
Clear	Edit Clear	Del
Copy	Edit Copy	Ctrl-Insert
Create a Book	File Book	Alt-F B
Cut	Edit Cut	Shift-Del
Document New	File New	Ctrl-N
Document Open	File Open	Ctrl-O
Document Print	File Print	Ctrl-P

Quick Guide to Application Commands

Function	Menu Option	Key Sequence
Document Save	File Save	Ctrl-S
Document Save As	File Save As	Alt-F A
Document Setup	File Page Setup	Alt-F G
Help	Help	F1
Indents and Tabs	Type Indents/Tabs	Ctrl-I
Insert a Bullet		Ctrl-Shift-8
Insert a Copyright		Ctrl-Shift-0 (zero)
Insert a Page Number		Ctrl-Shift-3
Insert a Trademark		Ctrl-Shift-G
Insert Another File	File Place	Ctrl-D
Page Display 25%	Page 25% Size	Ctrl-0 (zero)
Page Display 50%	Page 50% Size	Ctrl-5
Page Display 75%	Page 75% Size	Ctrl-7
Page Display 100%	Page Actual Size	Ctrl-1
Page Display 200%	Page 200% Size	Ctrl-2
Page Display 400%	Page 400% Size	Ctrl-4
Page Display Window	Page Fit in Window	Ctrl-W
Page Display World	Shift-Page Fit in Window	Shift-Ctrl-W
Page Go To	Page Go to Page	Ctrl-G
Page Insert	Page Insert Pages	Alt-P I
Page Remove	Page Remove Pages	Alt-P R
Paragraph Format	Type Paragraph	Ctrl-M
Paste	Edit Paste	Shift-Insert
Story Editor	Edit Edit Story	Ctrl-E

Function	Menu Option	Key Sequence
Story Editor Change	Edit Change	Ctrl-9
Story Editor Find	Edit Find	Ctrl-8
Story Editor Find Next	Edit Find Next	Shift-Ctrl-9
Story Editor Spelling	Edit Spelling	Ctrl-L
Text Bold		F6
Text Italic		F7
Text Larger by One Point Size		Ctrl-Shift->
Text Normal		F5
Text Reverse		Ctrl-Shift-V
Text Smaller by One Point Size		Ctrl-Shift-<
Text Underline		F8
Type Specifications	Type Type Specs	Ctrl-T

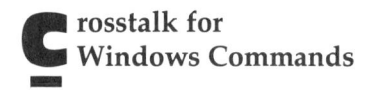

Crosstalk for Windows Commands

The following are commonly used Crosstalk for Windows commands. Each function is listed with its menu option and keystrokes.

Function	Menu Option	Key Sequence
Auto Answer Mode	Actions Scripts [Auto Answer] Run	Alt-A S [*highlight Auto Answer*] R
COM Port Settings	Setup Device	Alt-S D [*make selections*]
Dial Out	Actions Dial [Phone Number] Dial	Alt-A [*highlight desired phonebook entry*] D

Quick Guide to Application Commands 191

Function	Menu Option	Key Sequence
Disconnect	Actions Disconnect	Alt-A D
Exit Program	File Exit	Alt-F X
Modem Settings	Setup Modem	Alt-S M [*make selections*]
New Phonebook Entry	File New [Settings] OK	Alt-F N [*enter information*] <Return>
Open a Phonebook Entry	File Open [Entry] Open	Alt-F O [*highlight desired entry*] <Return>
Password Settings	Setup Session Password	Alt-S S P [*enter password*]
Receive Information	File Receive [Files] OK	Alt-F R [*select file(s)*] <Return>
Send Information	File Send [Files] OK	Alt-F S [*select file(s)*] <Return>
Terminal Emulation	Setup Terminal	Alt-S T [*make selection*]
Transfer Protocol	Setup Protocol	Alt-S P [*make selection*]

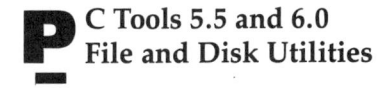

PC Tools 5.5 and 6.0 File and Disk Utilities

The following sections describe how to use some of PC Tools utilities. They include instructions for six utilities:

- COMPRESS
- DISKFIX
- MIRROR
- PCBACKUP
- PCCACHE
- REBUILD

COMPRESS

COMPRESS defragments your hard disk. See Chapter 3 for a description of defragmentation.

To start COMPRESS:

Type **COMPRESS** and press the Return key at the DOS prompt.

To test for disk fragmentation (does not defragment your disk):

Mouse
1. Pull down the Analysis menu.
2. Select Disk Analysis.

Keyboard
1. Press Alt-A to see the Analysis menu.
2. Press **D** to select Disk Analysis.

To test for disk fragmentation:

Mouse
1. Pull down the Compress menu.
2. Select Begin Compress.
3. If necessary, during the compression process, halt the program by pressing the F3 function key.
4. At the warning, click on Continue to continue or Exit to exit.

Keyboard
1. Press Alt-C to see the Compress menu.
2. Press **B** to select Begin Compress.
3. Same as mouse.
4. At the warning, press **C** to continue or **X** to exit.

DISKFIX

DISKFIX scans a specified disk for possible problems such as lost clusters, missing data, and problems in the FAT. Use this utility if you have problems reading and writing data to a disk.

To start DISKFIX:

At the DOS prompt, type **DISKFIX** and press the Return key.

To use DISKFIX:

1. DISKFIX will prompt you for the letter of the drive to fix. Enter a letter (such as C) as requested.

2. DISKFIX will check for a corrupted DOS boot sector, a bad FAT, lost clusters, and other problems.

3. As DISKFIX discovers problems, it will ask if you want them fixed. Respond Yes or No as appropriate.

4. When DISKFIX indicates that testing has been completed, press Return to continue.

5. Respond Y (Yes) when DISKFIX asks if you want to search for lost directories.

6. Respond Y (Yes) when it asks if you want to check the media surface.

7. Respond Y or N (Yes or No) as appropriate when it asks if you want to print a report of the results.

8. Select the Exit to DOS menu item to exit the program, or choose another option.

MIRROR

MIRROR produces a copy of your hard disk's file allocation table (FAT), root directory listing, and boot sector so that you can recover the data if necessary. It is good practice to put the MIRROR command in your AUTOEXEC.BAT file so that a new copy of your disk's information will be created each time you start your computer.

To start MIRROR:

At the DOS prompt, type **MIRROR** and press the Return key.

To start MIRROR with delete tracker (which allows you to recover files more reliably), use the /T parameter:

At the DOS prompt, type **MIRROR /TC** and press Return (substitute the appropriate drive letter for **C** if you want to mirror another drive).

PCBACKUP

PCBACKUP produces an archive (backup copy) of selected hard disk files on either a floppy disk or tape cartridge.

To start PCBACKUP:

At the DOS prompt, type **PCBACKUP** and press the Return key.

To back up all files on the hard disk:

Mouse	Keyboard
1. Pull down the Backup menu.	1. Press Alt-B to see the Backup menu.
2. Select Start backup.	2. Press **S** to start.
3. Insert diskettes when prompted.	3. Same as mouse.

Quick Guide to Application Commands 195

To select directories and files you do not want backed up:

Mouse

1. Pull down the Backup menu.

2. Select Choose Directories.

3. In the Tree window, use the arrow keys to highlight a directory you do *not* want to back up and press Return to select it, or press Tab to move to the file list and use the arrow keys and press Return to select the files you do *not* want to back up.

4. Repeat step 3 for all unwanted directories and files.

Keyboard

1. Press Alt-B to see the Backup menu.

2. Press **H** to select Choose Directories.

3. Same as mouse.

4. Same as mouse.

To restore files from floppy disk or tape to a hard drive:

Mouse

1. Pull down the Restore menu.

2. Select Start Restore.

3. Insert your backup floppy disks when prompted.

4. If necessary, cancel the Restore command while it is in progress by pressing the F3 function key.

Keyboard

1. Press Alt-R to see the Restore menu.

2. Press **S** to select Start Restore.

3. Same as mouse.

4. Same as mouse.

196 The Laptop User's Survival Guide

To save your backup settings:

Mouse

1. Pull down the Options menu.
2. Select Save Setup.
3. Type a setup file name when prompted and press Return.

Keyboard

1. Press Alt-O to see the Options menu.
2. Press **S** to select Save Setup.
3. Same as mouse.

To load your backup settings:

Mouse

1. Pull down the Options menu.
2. Select Load Setup.
3. Use the arrow keys to select a setup file and press Return.

Keyboard

1. Press Alt-O to see the Options menu.
2. Press **L** to select Load Setup.
3. Same as mouse.

PCCACHE

PCCACHE creates a disk cache using extended, expanded, or conventional memory. See Chapter 12 for more information about disk caches. Note that you should never use PCCACHE with other disk-cache utilities, such as Smartdrive (a Windows utility).

To start PCCACHE:

At the DOS prompt, type **PCCACHE** and press the Return key.

Optionally, you can add the following options after the PCCACHE command:

/?   Displays help on setting various PCCACHE parameters.

Quick Guide to Application Commands 197

/EXTSTART = *nnnn*K Specifies the starting address of the cache in extended memory. The address, *nnnn*, must be greater than 1024.

/FLUSH Clears all information from the cache.

/I*x* Tells PCCACHE to ignore drive *x*, so that it does not keep any information from that drive in the cache. This option is most frequently used for floppy disk drives (typically drives A: and B:).

/INFO Displays drives and the cache size available to each.

/MAX = *nn* Specifies the maximum number of sectors that can be stored in the cache during a single read request.

/MEASURES Displays performance and speed improvements resulting from the use of PCCACHE.

/PARAM Displays all current PCCACHE settings.

/SIZE = *nnn*K Specifies the size of the cache. For example, the command PCCACHE \SIZE = 256K sets the size of the cache to 256K.

/SIZEXP = *nnn*K Specifies the amount of expanded memory to be used by PCCACHE.

/SIZEXT = *nnn*K Specifies the amount of extended memory to be used by PCCACHE.

/UNLOAD Clears the cache and unloads PCCACHE from memory.

/WRITE = *nn* Specifies a delay of *nn* before write requests are sent to disk.

REBUILD

REBUILD automatically uses information stored in the file created by the MIRROR command to rebuild a disk that has had its information removed by the FORMAT command.

To start REBUILD and have it rebuild your disk:

At the DOS prompt, type **REBUILD** and press the Return key.

APPENDIX A

Guide to Product Sources

This appendix lists sources for the products mentioned in this book.

Cases

Lappac
Targus
Buena Park, CA
Phone: (714)523-5429

Tenba Computer Traveller
Quality Cases Limited
New York, NY
Phone: (212)966-1013

Communication Software

Carbon Copy
Microcom
500 River Ridge Drive
Norwood, MA 02062
Phone: (800)372-0200 or (617)551-1000

Crosstalk, Crosstalk for Windows
DCA
1000 Holcomb Woods Parkway #440
Roswell, GA 30076
Phone: (404)998-3998

MTEZ
Magicsoft
P.O. Box 396
Lombard, IL 60148
Phone: (708)953-2374

pcANYWHERE
DMA
1776 East Jericho Turnpike
Huntington, NY 11743
Phone: (516)462-0440

Reach Out
Ocean Isle Software
730 14th Street
Vero Beach, FL 32960
Phone: (407)770-4777

LANLink
Software Link
3577 Parkwat Lane
Norcross, GA 30092
Phone: (800)451-5465

LANtastic
Artisoft
575 East River Road
Tucson, AZ 85704
Phone: (602)293-6363

Connectivity

KONNEX
Unlimited Systems Corporation, Inc.
9225 Chesapeake Drive, Suite J
San Diego, CA 92123
Phone: (619)277-3300
Fax: (619)277-3305

Telcoupler/CP + Connection
Computer Products Plus
163 Gothard Street
Huntington Beach, CA 92647
Phone: (714)847-1799

Database Software

dBASE
Ashton-Tate
20101 Hamilton Avenue
Torrance, CA 90502
Phone: (213)329-8000

Paradox
Borland International, Inc.
P.O. Box 660001
Scotts Valley, CA 95067-0001
Phone: (800)345-2888 or (408)438-5300

FoxPro
Fox Software
134 W. South Boundary
Perrysburgh, OH 43551
Phone: (419)874-0162

Desktop Publishing Software

Ventura Publisher
Xerox Corporation
15175 Innovation Drive
San Diego, CA 92128
Phone: (800)228-8579 or (619)673-0172

PageMaker
Aldus Corporation
411 First Avenue South
Seattle, WA 98104-2871
Phone: (206)622-5500

Graphics Software

Corel Draw
Corel Systems Corporation
Ottawa, Ontario KIZ 8R7
Phone: (613)728-8200
Fax: (613)728-9790

Micrographix Designer
Micrographix, Inc.
1303 Arapaho
Richardson, TX 75081
Phone: (214)234-1769

LAN Boards and Adapters

Megahertz Corporation
4505 South Wasatch Boulevard
Salt Lake City, UT 84124
Phone: (801)272-6000

Puredata
1740 South I-35
Carrollton, TX 75006
Phone: (214)242-2040

pLan Adapter
IQ Technologies
22032 23rd Drive SE
Bothell, WA 98021
Phone: (800)227-2817

Pocket LAN Adapter
Xircom
Calabases, CA
Phone: (818)884-8755

Memory Managers

QEMM
Quarterdeck Office Systems
150 Pico Boulevard
Santa Monica, CA 90405
Phone: (213)392-9701

Modems and Fax Modems

Hayes 9600b Modem
Hayes Micro Computer Products Inc.
Norcross, GA
Phone: (404)441-1616

SatisFAXtion
Intel Corporation
5200 Northeast Elam Young Parkway
Hillsboro, OR 97124
Phone: (800)525-3019

WorldPort 2496
Touchbase Systems, Inc.
160 Laurel Avenue
Northport, NY 11768
Phone: (516)261-0423

Operating Systems

MS-DOS Version 5.0
Microsoft Corporation
One Microsoft Way
Redmond, WA 98052-6399
Phone: (206)882-8080

Windows
Microsoft Corporation
One Microsoft Way
Redmond, WA 98052-6399
Phone: (206)882-8080

Pointing Devices

Ballpoint Mouse
Microsoft Corporation
One Microsoft Way
Redmond, WA 98052-6399
Phone: (206)882-8080

TrackMan Portable
Logitech Corporation
6505 Kaiser Drive
Fremont, CA 94555
Phone: (510)795-8500

Portable Scanning Devices

Scanman Model 32
Logitech Corporation
6505 Kaiser Drive
Fremont, CA 94555
Phone: (510)795-8500

M800
Marstek, Inc.
17795-F Sky Park Circle
Irvine, CA 92714
Phone: (714)833-7740

Spreadsheet Software

Excel
Microsoft Corporation
One Microsoft Way
Redmond, WA 98052-6399
Phone: (206)882-8080

Lotus 1-2-3
Lotus Development Corporation
55 Cambridge Parkway
Cambridge, MA 02142
Phone: (617)577-8500

Supplies

Global Computer Products
2318 East Del Amo Boulevard
Department 22
Compton, CA 90220
Phone: (800)845-6225
Fax: (213)637-6191

Type Managers

Adobe Type Manager
Adobe Systems Inc.
1585 Charleston Road
Mountain View, CA 94039
Phone: (800)344-8335 or (415)962-4809

Facelift
Bitstream, Inc.
215 First Street
Cambridge, MA 02142
Phone: (800)522-3668 or (617)497-6222

Utilities

The Brooklyn Bridge
Fifth Generation Systems
Baton Rouge, LA
Phone: (800)873-4384

Fast Lynx
Rupp Corp
New York, NY
Phone: (800)852-7877

LapLink III or *WinConnect*
Traveling Software
Bothell, WA
Phone: (800)662-2652

Mace Utilities
Fifth Generation Systems
10049 North Reiger Road
Baton Rouge, LA 70809
Phone: (800)873-4384

The Norton Utilities
Peter Norton Computing Inc.
100 Wilshire Boulevard, 9th Floor
Santa Monica, CA 90401-1104
Phone: (213)319-2010

PC Tools
Central Point Software
Beaverton, OR
Phone: (503)690-8090

PKZIP
PKWare
Glendale, WI
Phone: (414)352-3670

Word Processing Software

Microsoft Word
Microsoft Corporation
One Microsoft Way
Redmond, WA 98052-6399
Phone: (206)882-8080

WordPerfect
WordPerfect Corporation
1555 N. Technology Way
Orem, UT 84057
Phone: (800)526-5011

APPENDIX B

Glossary of Terms

acoustic coupler: A device to attach a modem to a telephone. It has special cups into which a telephone handset can be placed or connected.

ANSI: Stands for the *American National Standards Institute*. An organization that specifies computer standards.

ANSI.SYS: A software driver that allows you to take greater advantage of your monitor in character mode. ANSI.SYS must be loaded from your **CONFIG.SYS** file.

ASCII: Stands for *American Standard Code for Information Interchange*. A set of 127 standard letters, numbers, punctuation symbols, and some special marks. The IBM PC character set extends this character set to 255 characters.

AUTOEXEC.BAT: A file that automatically executes when you start your computer. This file is known as a **batch file.**

baud: A measure of transmission speed equivalent to the number of bits per second that can be transmitted. The baud rate is not exactly the same as bits per second, but with asynchronous transmission, the baud rate and bits per second are approximately equal.

batch file: A file containing one or more MS-DOS commands. Batch files are useful for executing a series of commands in a batch without having to type in each command individually. The **AUTOEXEC.BAT** file is an example of a batch file.

bit: From the words *binary digit*. An electronic signal or piece of data, or a number which is viewed as having exactly two states: on or off, one or zero, yes or no. Bits are used in electronic computer systems to encode orders (instructions) and data. Bits are usually grouped in **bytes** (eight or nine bits). A megabit is one million bits; a kilobit is one thousand bits.

bus: A circuit or group of circuits that provides an electronic pathway between two or more microprocessors or input/output devices, such as a

Glossary of Terms

video board and CPU. The bigger this pathway, the more information can be processed at one time. Most PCs have either a 16-bit or 32-bit bus.

byte: A collection of eight (sometimes nine) **bits** that, when taken together, represent a piece of information in machine language or a program instruction.

CCITT V.42 protocol: Used as an error-control protocol for **modem** transmissions.

central processing unit: See **CPU**.

CGA: See **graphics adapter**.

chip: A group of electronic circuits that performs a few to a large number of functions. These electronic circuits are manufactured and put into a chip of silicon about ¼-inch square. A computer chip can be placed into a specific area on a printed circuit board in the computer.

CONFIG.SYS: A system file that is automatically read by MS-DOS when your computer is started. The file normally loads device drivers into memory for use by your system and applications.

CPU: Stands for *central processing unit*. This is the portion of the computer that interprets the program and does arithmetic and logical operations. In a microcomputer, the CPU is contained on a single microprocessor chip on a printed circuit board. All IBM-compatible personal computers are based on the Intel series of microprocessors (8088, 8086, 80286, 80386, 80486).

device driver: A software program used to perform a variety of standard computer functions, such as handling mouse input, managing memory, and sending output to a printer. This program is loaded into your computer's memory when you turn on your computer.

dpi: Stands for *dots per inch*. Used as the measurement for the density level or resolution of printed material. Most dot-matrix printers have a resolution of 150 dpi. Typically, 200 dpi is acceptable for business correspondence; 300 dpi is acceptable for most newspaper printing; and 2400 dpi is suitable for magazine on glossy stock.

EGA: See **graphics adapter.**

expanded memory: A type of memory that allows your computer to have more than the standard 640K of conventional memory. Expanded memory uses portions of the 384K area between conventional and **extended memory.** To use expanded memory, a computer must have a special expanded memory card and **device driver.** Expanded memory has been replaced by extended memory in some cases.

expansion chassis: A device that extends the number of **expansion slots** available to a computer. An expansion chassis usually connects to a computer through a ribbon cable and offers from two to eight additional slots into which boards can be inserted.

expansion slot: A berth inside your computer that is used to hold printed circuit boards. For example, a **fax-modem** board can be plugged into an empty expansion slot.

extended memory: Memory in addition to conventional memory that is not readily accessible to MS-DOS or MS-DOS applications. Extended memory cannot be used on 8086/8088 computers. This memory resides above the 1 megabyte boundary and can be accessed by extended memory applications through the **HIMEM.SYS** device driver.

FAT: Stands for *file allocation table.* An area of your hard disk that stores a hard disk's directory structure and other information.

fax modem: A device that can be used by your computer to send and receive facsimile images and to send and receive files over the telephone lines.

file allocation table: See **FAT.**

file format: The structure or arrangement of data stored in a file.

fileserver: A central hub for a **network** of computers. It is the core of the system, which allows information and devices to be shared and polices activities performed by computers tied into the network.

filter: A utility built into an application to provide conversion between its own internal format and some other file format.

font cartridge: A piece of hardware that is plugged into a printer to supply one or more fonts.

graphics adapter: A device or card placed in the computer that controls images and resolution on a computer monitor. MDA stands for *monochrome display adapter;* CGA stands for *color graphics adapter;* EGA stands for *enhanced graphics adapter;* and VGA stands for *video graphics adapter.*

hard disk: A data (program or information) storage device that can be accessed by the computer. Often, this is called hard disk memory. Hard disk memory is not lost when the computer is turned off.

HIMEM.SYS: A device driver that manages how applications access and use **extended memory**. The HIMEM.SYS driver is loaded from the **CONFIG.SYS** file when the computer is started.

HPPCL: Stands for *Hewlett-Packard Printer Control Language.* It is a standard format for data that is sent to a printer.

LAN: Stands for *local area network.* See also **network**.

LAP-M protocol: An error-control protocol for **modem** transmissions.

MB: Stands for *megabyte.* It equals 1,024,000 bytes of memory.

MDA: See **graphics adapter.**

memory manager: A software program that handles **extended** or **expanded memory** (or both). Memory managers are normally loaded from the **CONFIG.SYS** file. They can also provide more conventional memory for MS-DOS applications.

MNP 2–4 protocol: An error-detection and correction protocol for **modem** transmissions.

modem: From *modulator/demodulator.* A device that allows your computer to send and receive information over the telephone lines.

motherboard: The main printed circuit board inside your computer that usually holds the **CPU, RAM,** and other key system components.

network: A group of machines tied together so that information and devices can be shared. For example, a **LAN** represents computers that are physically tied together through some type of transmission medium.

network card: A computer board that fits into a computer's **expansion slot.** It allows for transmission through some type of cable, connecting the computer with the **network.** Network cards vary in design (topology) and speed (transfer rate).

outline font: A font that is specified by a mathematical formula instead of a group of bits. Outline fonts may be scaled to any dimension through the use of a **type manager.**

parallel port: A communications port on your computer that allows for the transmission of information from your computer to a variety of devices, including printers and external drives. Parallel ports transmit data one byte (eight bits) at a time.

PCX format: One of several widely used file formats for graphic images.

peer-to-peer network: A **network** that does not have a central information point (**fileserver**). Instead, data and devices are spread out through the machines connected together.

Glossary of Terms   215

PostScript: A page-description language specified by Adobe Systems and used on a wide variety of printers and other output devices. It is similar to **HPPCL** but provides additional functions. Before sending output to a PostScript-compatible device, an application must use a special driver to format the information in PostScript format.

printer font: A font that resides in your printer's memory and is generated at the time your document is printed.

RAM: Stands for *random-access memory*. RAM is solid-state, electronic data storage that can send and receive information quickly. Programs are loaded into RAM when you run them. This memory is lost when the computer is turned off.

ROM: Stands for *read-only memory*. ROM is like RAM, but the information stored in ROM chips is not lost when you turn off your computer. ROM is also used to store information about your computer's hardware.

RS-232:   A widely used communications standard. Many computers use the RS-232 standard for serial communications.

RTF format: Stands for *Rich Text Format*. RTF is a widely used file format for exchanging information between word processors and other applications on MS-DOS, MS-OS2, and Macintosh computers.

serial port: A communications port on your computer that sends and receives information one bit at a time. Serial ports are typically used for **modem** and printer connections.

soft font: A font that is downloaded from your computer to your printer when needed.

swap file: An area of the hard disk used by Windows as a substitute for **RAM** if it runs out of RAM. This is also known as **virtual memory.**

tape backup: A cassette tape system that can hold a copy of information stored on your computer. Backups usually are needed if a problem develops with the original.

TIFF: Stands for *Tagged Image File Format*. A widely used standard that specifies the format of graphical (image) information.

TSR: Stands for *terminate and stay resident*. A TSR is a utility that remains in memory while other programs are running. An example of a TSR is a screen-grabber utility that stays in memory and allows you to capture the contents on the screen while another program is running.

type manager: A software package that handles your systems fonts, allowing you to scale them to any size and use them with a variety of output devices.

transfer rate: The speed at which information is transferred from one device to another. The customary units are kilobits (K/sec) or megabits (Mb/sec) per second.

VGA: See **graphics adapter.**

virtual memory: A memory management system used by programs such as Windows that are running in 80386 protected mode. With virtual memory, your system can use disk memory as a substitute for **RAM**.

virus: A program that is able to distribute itself from one system to another by a variety of means that are undetected by the user.

WYSIWYG: Stands for *what you see is what you get*. Used to describe a screen display that matches the printed output.

APPENDIX C

Creating Traveling Versions of Your Applications

This appendix lists application files that you may want to remove from your hard disk to conserve space. These are files that are not critical for your use of the application and may not be necessary for your laptop computing on the road.

Noncritical files and subdirectories, the disk space they consume (in kilobytes), and the functions you will lose by deleting them are listed for the following applications:

- WordPerfect
- MS Word for Windows
- MS Word for DOS
- Lotus 1-2-3
- Excel for Windows
- PageMaker for Windows
- PC Tools

Chapter 2 of this book lists the files you may want to remove from MS-DOS and Windows.

Before deleting a file or subdirectory, be sure that you will not need to use it. This appendix gives you an idea of the circumstances under which you would want to remove the file or files. In general, you should run the application tutorials and look through the samples before deleting those files. If you need more information before making the decision, consult your software's documentation.

Instead of deleting the files, you may want to compress them with PKZIP (or another compression utility) and store them in compressed form. Then if you find that you do need one of the files, you can decompress it by using PKUNZIP. See Chapters 2 and 5 of this book for more information about compression utilities.

WordPerfect 5.1

LEARN	278K	Remove the files in the WP\LEARN directory if you do not need to run the tutorial.
*.WPG	73K	Remove the files with the extension WPG if you do not need to work with graphics files.
*.WPM	175K	Remove the files with the extension WPM if you do not need to run macros.

MS Word for Windows 1.1

.DOT files **except** NORMAL.DOT	320K	Remove the files in the WINWORD directory with the extension DOT if you do not need the templates. You can delete all the .DOT files but NORMAL.DOT.
SAMPLES	162K	Remove the files in the WINWORD\LIBRARY\SAMPLES directory if you do not need the samples.

MS Word for DOS 5.5

LEARN.EXE	115K	Remove if you do not need to run the tutorial.
MACROCNV.EXE	105K	Remove if you do not need to convert macro files from Word 5.0 to Word 5.5 format.
MAKEPRD.EXE	61K	Remove if you do not need to modify the capabilities of your printer drivers (rarely done).

MAKEVID.EXE	8K	Remove if you do not need to modify the capabilities of your video drivers (rarely done).
MERGEPRD.EXE	126K	Remove if you do not need to modify the capabilities of your printer drivers (rarely done).
MSD.EXE	64K	Remove if you do not need the utility that provides information about your system, such as the BIOS version and the operating system version.
RIBBON.SCR	50K	Remove if you do not use any of the sample files supplied with the program.
WORDONE.*	155K	Remove if you do not need to run the tutorial.
WORDTWO.*	167K	Remove if you do not need to run the tutorial.

Lotus 1-2-3 2.3

*.DOC	60K	Remove if you do not need the sample documents and information.
TUTOR	1470K	Remove if you do not need to run the tutorial.
WYSIWYG	2310K	Remove if you do not need to run in What You See Is What You Get mode for the spreadsheet.
WYSYGO	1070K	Remove if you do not need to run in What You See Is What You Get mode for graphics.

Creating Traveling Versions of Your Applications

Lotus 1-2-3 3.1

WYSIWYG	1200K	Remove if you do not need to run in What You See Is What You Get mode.

Excel for Windows 2.1c

EXCELCBT	1000K	Remove the files in the EXCEL\EXCELCBT directory if you do not need to run the tutorial.
EXCELDE.EXE	87K	Remove if you do not use the dialog editor to create custom dialog boxes for macros.
LIBRARY	389K	Remove the files in the EXCEL\LIBRARY directory if you do not need the samples.
TRANS*.*	125K	Remove if you do not need to translate Lotus 1-2-3 or Multiplan macros to Excel macros.

PageMaker for Windows 4.0

AVERY	66K	Remove the files in the PM4\TEMPLATE\AVERY directory if you do not need the sample mailing label templates.
GRIDS	72K	Remove the files in the PM4\TEMPLATE\GRIDS directory if you do not need the sample grid templates.
TEMPLATE	832K	Remove the files in the PM4\TEMPLATE directory if you do not need any of the sample templates.

PC Tools 7.0

PSECURE.EXE	109K	Remove if you do not need to prevent others from accessing your laptop's files.
SAMPLES	124K	Remove the files in the PCTOOLS\SAMPLES directory if you do not need them to learn how to use the VIEWER program.
WIPE.EXE	101K	Remove if you do not need to wipe data off your disk completely.

INDEX

A

acoustic couplers, 114, 127–128
adapters
    external LAN, 99–100, 204
    plug, 9–10
Adobe Type Manager, 67, 207
airports
    security checks in, 130–131
    working in, 129–130, 145
APPEND command (DOS), 149
application swap files, 36–37
application windows, Windows key sequences for, 165–166
application-specific data, exchanging, 40–41
archive files, 34, 54–55
ARCnet network interface cards, 14
ASCII format
    for faxes, 116, 118–119
    for importing files, 41–42
ASSIGN command (DOS), 149
ASSIST command (dBASE), 183
ATTRIB command (DOS), 149
AUTOEXEC.BAT files, customizing, 23

B

BACKUP command (DOS), 149–150
Backup program, 143

backups, files, 14, 149–150
    with PC Tools, 141, 143, 194–196
    for RAM disk data, 141
    selective, 141
    strategy for, 142–144
Ballpoint Mouse, 6–7, 205
batch files, 22–23
battery packs
    prolonging life of, 137–141
    spare, 4–5
bit-map fonts, 64, 66–67
BREAK command (DOS), 150
broadcast fax messages, 112
Brooklyn Bridge transfer utility, 55, 73, 98, 207
BROWSE command (dBASE), 183
buffering techniques in modems, 87
bulletin board services
    for faxes, 119–120
    OAG Electronic Edition Travel Service, 144–146

C

cables
    for file transfers, 72, 74
    for floppy disks, 11–12
    for modems, 3–4, 126–127
    for monitors, 25
    for printing, 10–11, 60–61

Carbon Copy program, 90, 200
cartridges, printer, 68
cases
    benefits of, 15
    sources for, 200
CD command (DOS), 150
cell formatting keystrokes for Excel, 181–182
CHCP command (DOS), 150
CHKDSK command (DOS), 151
Cleanup virus checker, 56
CLS command (DOS), 151
commands
    Crosstalk, 190–191
    dBASE, 183–188
    DOS, 148–163
    Excel, 177–182
    Lotus 1-2-3, 175–177
    PageMaker, 188–190
    Windows, 163–167
    Word, 171–175
    WordPerfect, 167–171
communications. *See* remote communications
COMP command (DOS), 151
comparing files, 151, 153–154
COMPRESS utility (PC Tools), 192
compressing files
    for backups, 142
    fax files, 122
    with Save As command, 30–31
    for traveling versions of applications, 218
    utilities for, 34, 54–55

compression, modems with, 86–90
CONFIG.SYS file
    for RAM disks, 140
    removing device drivers from, 22–23
configuration for remote communications, 78–79
connectivity
    for networks, 96
    for remote communications, 78–79
    software sources for, 201–202
contiguous files, 33–34, 54, 192
conversion utilities, 57
converting fax documents, 120–121
COPY command (DOS), 142–143, 151–152
COPY FILE command (dBASE), 183
COPY STRUCTURE TO command (dBASE), 183
copying files, 134, 142–143, 151–153, 162–163, 183
cords, power, 2–3
CP+ Connection device, 128–129, 202
CRC (cyclical redundancy check) error control, 85
CREATE command (dBASE), 184
CREATE REPORT command (dBASE), 184
Crosstalk software package, 90
    commands in, 190–191
    source for, 200

Index **225**

cursor movement keys for Excel, 177–178

D

databases
  compressing, 55
  exchange formats for, 45
  sources for, 202
  standard application for, 46
DATE command (DOS), 152
dBASE database manager
  commands for, 183–188
  source for, 202
DEBUG.COM file, disk space used by, 32
defragmenting files, 33–34, 54, 192
DEL command (DOS), 152
DELETE command (dBASE), 184
deleted files, recovering, 53, 161–162
demo files, removing, 33
desktop computers, remote control of, 90–94
desktop faxes, 107, 112–113
Desktop Flight Guide, 144–146
desktop publishing software, sources for, 202–203
device drivers, removing, 22–23
dialing codes for remote communications, 93
dialog boxes, Windows key sequences for, 166–167
DIR command (dBASE), 184
DIR command (DOS), 152–153

directories, mirrored, 73–74
disk caches, 139, 196–197
DISKCOMP command (DOS), 153
DISKCOPY command (DOS), 153
DISKFIX utility (PC Tools), 193
disk-intensive work, AC power for, 141
disks, RAM, 139–141. *See also* floppy disks; hard disks
DISPLAY STATUS command (dBASE), 184
DO command (dBASE), 184
document layout, standard application for, 46
DOS
  commands in, 148–163
  memory management by, 21
  removing unnecessary files from, 31–32
  source for, 205
  utilities in, 50–51
  version 5.0, 51–52
DOSKEY utility (DOS), 52
drivers, printer, 62–64

E

EDIT command (DOS), 153
EDLIN command (DOS), 153
EJECT command (dBASE), 185
electrical outlets, 2–3, 125–126
EMM386.SYS file, disk space used by, 31–32
Encapsulated PostScript format, 41

environments
    hostile, 124–131
    laptop, 18–19
error control
    with backups, 143
    modems with, 85–86, 89–90
Ethernet network interface
    cards, 14
Excel for Windows spreadsheet
    program
        commands in, 177–182
        source for, 206
        traveling version of, 221
exchanging files
    conversion utilities for, 57
    exporting, 43
    and floppy disk compatibility, 73, 134–136
    fonts, 46–47
    formats for, 41–45
    importing, 41–42
    for mirrored directories, 73–74
    sharing, 40–41
    transfer utilities for, 55, 72–75, 136
EXIT command (DOS), 154
expansion chassis
    for connectivity, 79
    for networks, 100–101
expansion slots
    limitations on, 19
    uses for, 26–28, 79–80
exporting files, 43
extended memory, 20–21
extension cords, 3

external devices
    fax modems, 8, 28, 109–110, 114
    hard disk drives, 143
    LAN adapters, 99–100
    modems, 81
    monitors, 25–26
    pocket faxes, 28

F

Facelift type manager, 67, 207
Fast Lynx transfer utility, 55, 98, 207
Fastback Plus program, 143
FASTOPEN command (DOS), 154
faxes and fax modems, 7–9, 106
    broadcast messages with, 112
    bulletin board services for, 119–120
    desktop, 107, 112–113
    expansion slots for, 26, 79–80
    external, 28, 109–110, 114
    internal, 108–110, 114
    portable, 108, 114
    printer redirection with, 112, 115–119
    receiving, 120–122
    scanners for, 115
    scheduled transmissions with, 111
    sources for, 204–205
FC command (DOS), 154
FDISK command (DOS), 31, 154
File menu (Windows), 163

Index **227**

files
  backing up, 14, 141–144, 149–150, 194–196
  comparing, 151, 153–154
  compressing, 30–31, 34, 54–55, 122, 142, 218
  conversion utilities for, 57
  copying, 134, 151–153, 162–163, 183
  deleting, 152
  displaying contents of, 161
  exchanging (*See* exchanging files)
  fragmented, 33–34, 54, 192
  listing, 152–153
  locating, 53
  protecting, 56
  recovering, 53, 156, 158, 161–162, 194
  renaming, 159
  replacing, 159
  restoring, 159
  swap, 35–37
  unnecessary, removing, 31–33
filters, file exchange, 41–42
FIND command (DOS), 154–155
flights, guide for, 144–146
floppy disks
  backing up files to, 142–143
  compatibility of, 73, 134–136
  storing unnecessary files on, 31–33
  transfer programs for, 11–12
fonts
  exchanging, 46–47
  for printing, 66–68

FORMAT command (DOS), 155
formats and file exchange, 41–45
formatting disk, recovering from, 53, 162, 198
formula bar keystrokes for Excel, 179
fragmented files, 33–34, 54, 192
function keys for Excel, 180–181

G

General menu (Windows), 164–165
GOTO command (dBASE), 185
graphics
  exchange formats for, 44–45
  with faxes, 119
  printer memory for, 65
  software sources for, 203
  standard application for, 46
Group III fax format, 110, 116, 118, 120
GWBASIC.EXE file, disk space used by, 32

H

hand-held scanners, 115, 206
hard disks
  compressing files on, 30–31, 33–34, 54–55
  conserving space on, 31–33
  defragmenting files on, 33–34, 54–55, 192
  external, 143
  font space on, 68
  swap files on, 35–37

header and footer codes for Excel, 182
HELP command (DOS), 155
Help menu (Windows), 164
hostile environments
　airports, 129–131
　hotel rooms, 125–129
　preparing for, 124–125
hotel rooms, 125–129

I

importing files, 41–42
INDEX ON command (dBASE), 185
information resources, 144–146
interfaces
　for networks, 13–14, 101–102
　for printing, 62
internal modems and fax modems, 8, 81, 108–110, 114

J

JOIN command (DOS), 155

K

Kermit software package, 90
Konnexx device, 128–129, 201

L

LABEL command (DOS), 155
LANLink transfer utility, 98, 201
LANtastic package, 98, 201
LAP (Linked Access Packet)-M error control, 85

LapLink transfer utility, 55, 73–75, 136, 207
laser printers
　cables for, 11
　memory for, 64–65
Lempel-Ziv compression algorithm, 87
LHARC utility, 54, 89
LINK.EXE file, disk space used by, 32
LIST command (dBASE), 185–186
LIST STRUCTURE command (dBASE), 186
listing files, 152–153
local area networks. *See* networks
LOCATE command (dBASE), 186
Lotus 1-2-3 spreadsheet
　commands in, 175–177
　source for, 206
　traveling version of, 220–221

M

M800 scanner, 115, 206
Mace Utilities, 53–54, 207
mainframe computers, remote communications with, 91
MD command (DOS), 156
MEM command (DOS), 156
memory
　conserving, 22–23
　for disk caches, 139, 196–197
　expanding, 20–21
　expansion slots for, 27
　limitations on, 19
　for printing, 64–65
　for RAM disks, 139–141

Index

status of, 156
for zero-slot network packages, 97–98
memory managers, 21, 204
metal detectors, 130
MIRROR command (DOS), 51, 156
MIRROR utility (PC Tools), 194
mirrored directories, 73–74
MNP (Microcom Network Protocols)
    for data compression, 86–88
    for error control, 85–86
MODE command (DOS), 156–157
modems, 80
    cables for, 3–4, 126–127
    with data compression, 86–90
    with error control, 85–86, 89–90
    expansion slots for, 26, 79–80
    in faxes, 106
    internal, 81
    performance of, 83–85
    sources for, 204–205
MODIFY command (dBASE), 186
monitor boards, expansion slots for, 27
monitors
    limitations on, 19
    VGA with, 25–26
MORE command (DOS), 157
motel rooms, 125–129
mouse
    extra, 5–7
    and modems, 81–82
MTE communication package, 89–90

multiplexing by LAN adapters, 100

N

NetBIOS and zero-slot network approach, 97–98
network boards
    expansion slots for, 27, 79–80
    sources for, 203–204
networks, 12–14
    checklist for, 102–103
    expansion chassis for, 100–101
    external LAN adapters for, 99–100
    interface cards for, 101–102
    remote communications with, 91
    zero-slot approach to, 96–98
neutral data, exchanging, 41
NLSFUNC.EXE file, disk space used by, 32
Norton Utilities, 54
    for compressing files, 122
    for recovering files, 53
    for selective backups, 141
    source for, 208
notebook computers, xxvi

O

OAG Electronic Edition Travel Service, 130
OAG Travel Service, 145
OFFICE.BAT program, 24
operating systems, sources for, 205

Options menu (Windows), 164
outlets, electrical, 2–3, 125–126
outline fonts, 66–67

P

PACK command (dBASE), 186
page layout, printer memory for, 65
page setup control for printing, 66
PageMaker for Windows program
    commands for, 188–190
    source for, 203
    traveling version of, 221
palmtop computers, xxvi
partition tables, rebuilding, 51
pass-through by LAN adapters, 100
passwords for remote communications, 92
PATH command (DOS), 157
PBRUSH files, disk space used by, 32
PC Tools, 54, 191
    for backup files, 141, 143, 194–196
    for compressing files, 122, 192
    disk cache with, 139, 196–197
    for disk problems, 193
    for fragmented files, 33
    for recovering files, 53, 194, 198
    source for, 208
    traveling version of, 222
pcAnywhere program, 90, 201

PCBACKUP utility (PC Tools), 194–196
PCCACHE utility (PC Tools), 196–197
PCX format with faxes, 116, 120–121
permanent swap files, 35–36
PKZIP utility
    for backup files, 142–143
    for compressing files, 34, 54–55, 218
    for fax files, 122
    and modem compression, 89
    source for, 208
pLan LAN adapter, 100, 204
pocket faxes, 28
Pocket LAN Adapter, 100, 204
pocket-sized fax modems, 109–110
pointing devices
    extra, 5–7
    sources for, 205
portable computers, xxv
portable faxes, 108, 114
portable scanners, 115, 206
ports
    for modems, 81–83
    for remote communications, 91–92
PostScript cartridges, 68
power connections, adapters for, 9–10
power cords, 2–3
PRINT command (DOS), 158
printing
    cables for, 10–11, 60–61
    cartridges for, 68

Index **231**

drivers for, 62–64
equipment for, 60–61
to fax boards, 112, 115–119
for faxes, 113–114
fonts for, 66–68
interfaces for, 62
memory for, 64–65
page setup control for, 66
PROMPT command (DOS), 158
proprietary expansion slots, 26–27, 79–80
proprietary network cards, 101–102
protecting files, 56

Q

QEMM memory manager, 21, 204
QUIT command (dBASE), 186

R

RAM disks, 139–141
RD command (DOS), 159
Reach Out program, 91
Rebuild utility (DOS), 51
REBUILD utility (PC Tools), 198
RECORDER files, disk space used by, 32
RECOVER command (DOS), 158
recovering files, 53, 156, 158, 161–162, 194
REINDEX command (dBASE), 186–187
REM statement for CONFIG.SYS file, 22
remote communications
configuration for, 78–79
desktop control through, 90–94
expansion slots for, 79–80
fax modems for, 7–9
modems for, 80–86
software sources for, 200–201
REN command (DOS), 159
REPLACE command (DOS), 159
REPORT FORM command (dBASE), 187
RESTORE command (DOS), 159
REVERSI.EXE file, disk space used by, 32
ROAD.BAT program, 24
RTF format, 41

S

SatisFAXtion fax modem, 110, 115, 204
Save As command
for compressing files, 30–31
for exchanging files, 43
scalable fonts, 66–67
Scan virus checker, 56
Scanman Model 32 scanner, 115, 206
scanners, 115, 206
scheduled fax transmissions, 111
screen
fonts for, 67
power used by, 137–139
security for viruses, 56
SEEK command (dBASE), 187
SELECT command (DOS), 31, 159–160

selection keystrokes for Excel, 178–179
selective backups, 141
serial ports, expansion slots for, 80
SET command (dBASE), 187
SET command (DOS), 160
SETVER command (DOS), 160
SHARE.EXE file, disk space used by, 32
SHELL files, disk space used by, 32
slots
    limitations on, 19
    uses for, 26–28, 79–80
Smartdrive disk cache, 139
soft fonts for printing, 66–68
SOL.EXE file, disk space used by, 32
SORT command (DOS), 160
SPART.PAR file, 36
spreadsheets
    compressing, 55
    exchange formats for, 45
    printer memory for, 65
    sources for, 206
    standard application for, 46
    traveling versions of, 220–221
stand-alone faxes, 108, 114
SUBST command (DOS), 160
supplies, laptop computer, source for, 206
swap files, 35–37
SWAPFILE.EXE program, 36
SYS command (DOS), 161
system files, customizing, 23
system functions (Windows), 165

T

tape backup, expansion slots for, 27
TechSmith program, 91
Telecoupler acoustic coupler, 127
telephones
    cables for, 3–4, 126–127
    connectors for, 128–129
temporary swap files, 35
terminal settings for remote communications, 92
text-finding utilities, 53
3-to-2 plug adapters, 9–10
386SPART.PAR file, 36
TIFF format, 41
TIME command (DOS), 161
TrackMan Portable mouse, 6, 205
transfer protocols for remote communications, 92
transfer utilities, 11–12, 55, 72–75, 136
TREE command (DOS), 161
TYPE command (DOS), 161
type managers, 67–68, 207

U

UNDELETE command (DOS), 51, 161–162
UNFORMAT command (DOS), 162
uniformity for remote communications, 78–79
USE command (dBASE), 187
utilities
    in DOS, 50–51
    in PC Tools, 191–198

Index **233**

sources for, 207–208

V

V.22 transmission standard, 84
V.42 error control standard, 85–86
V.42bis data compression standard, 86–88
VER command (DOS), 162
VGA monitors, preparing for, 25–26
virtual memory, 35
viruses, protection from, 56
VOL command (DOS), 162

W

weather information, 145
WIN386.SWP file, 35
WinConnect transfer utility, 55
Window menu (Windows), 164
Windows
    disk caches in, 139
    fax printer redirection with, 116–117
    importing and exporting text with, 33
    memory use with, 20–21
    modems with, 81–83
    printer drivers in, 62
    printer fonts in, 68
    quick keys for, 163–167
    removing unnecessary files in, 32–33
    source for, 205
    swap files with, 35–37
    VGA with, 25–26

word processing
    compressing files from, 54–55
    exchange formats for, 44
    printer memory for, 65
    software sources for, 208
    standard application for, 46
    traveling versions of, 219–220
Word word processor
    commands in, 171–175
    filter for, 41
    source for, 208
    traveling versions of, 219–220
WordPerfect word processor
    commands in, 167–171
    filter for, 41
    printer definition for, 63
    source for, 208
    traveling version of, 219
WorldPort 2496 fax modem, 110, 118, 205
Write application (Windows), 33

X

x-ray machines, 130
XCOPY command (DOS), 162–163
XModem software package, 90

Y

YModem software package, 90

Z

ZAP command (dBASE), 187
zero-slot network packages, 96–98
ZModem software package, 90

Selections from The SYBEX Library

WORD PROCESSING

The ABC's of Microsoft Word (Third Edition)
Alan R. Neibauer
461pp. Ref. 604-9
This is for the novice WORD user who wants to begin producing documents in the shortest time possible. Each chapter has short, easy-to-follow lessons for both keyboard and mouse, including all the basic editing, formatting and printing functions. Version 5.0.

The ABC's of Microsoft Word for Windows
Alan R. Neibauer
334pp. Ref. 784-6
Designed for beginning Word for Windows users, as well as for experienced Word users who are changing from DOS to the Windows version. Covers everything from typing, saving, and printing your first document, to creating tables, equations, and graphics.

The ABC's of WordPerfect
Alan R. Neibauer
239pp. Ref. 425-9
This basic introduction to WordPefect consists of short, step-by-step lessons—for new users who want to get going fast. Topics range from simple editing and formatting, to merging, sorting, macros, and more. Includes version 4.2

The ABC's of WordPerfect 5
Alan R. Neibauer
283pp. Ref. 504-2
This introduction explains the basics of desktop publishing with WordPerfect 5: editing, layout, formatting, printing, sorting, merging, and more. Readers are shown how to use WordPerfect 5's new features to produce great-looking reports.

The ABC's of WordPerfect 5.1
Alan R. Neibauer
352pp. Ref. 672-3
Neibauer's delightful writing style makes this clear tutorial an especially effective learning tool. Learn all about 5.1's new drop-down menus and mouse capabilities that reduce the tedious memorization of function keys.

The Complete Guide to MultiMate
Carol Holcomb Dreger
208pp. Ref. 229-9
This step-by-step tutorial is also an excellent reference guide to MultiMate features and uses. Topics include search/replace, library and merge functions, repagination, document defaults and more.

Encyclopedia WordPerfect 5.1
Greg Harvey
Kay Yarborough Nelson
1100pp. Ref. 676-6
This comprehensive, up-to-date WordPerfect reference is a must for beginning

and experienced users alike. With complete, easy-to-find information on every WordPerfect feature and command—and it's organized by practical functions, with business users in mind.

Introduction to WordStar
Arthur Naiman
208pp. Ref. 134-9
This all time bestseller is an engaging first-time introduction to word processing as well as a complete guide to using WordStar—from basic editing to blocks, global searches, formatting, dot commands, SpellStar and MailMerge. Through Version 3.3.

Mastering Microsoft Word on the IBM PC (Fourth Edition)
Matthew Holtz
680pp. Ref. 597-2
This comprehensive, step-by-step guide details all the new desktop publishing developments in this versatile word processor, including details on editing, formatting, printing, and laser printing. Holtz uses sample business documents to demonstrate the use of different fonts, graphics, and complex documents. Includes Fast Track speed notes. For Versions 4 and 5.

Mastering Microsoft Word for Windows
Michael J. Young
540pp. Ref. 619-7
A practical introduction to Word for Windows, with a quick-start tutorial for newcomers. Subsequent chapters explore editing, formatting, and printing, and cover such advanced topics as page design, Style Sheets, the Outliner, Glossaries, automatic indexing, using graphics, and desktop publishing.

Mastering Microsoft Works on the IBM PC
Rebecca Bridges Altman
536pp. Ref. 690-1
Written especially for small business and home office users. Practical tutorials cover every aspect of word processing, spreadsheets, business graphics, database management and reporting, and basic telecommunications under Microsoft Works.

Mastering MultiMate 4.0
Paula B. Hottin
404pp. Ref. 697-9
Get thorough coverage from a practical perspective. Tutorials and real-life examples cover everything from first startup to basic editing, formatting, and printing; advanced editing and document management; enhanced page design, graphics, laser printing; merge-printing; and macros.

Mastering WordPerfect
Susan Baake Kelly
435pp. Ref. 332-5
Step-by-step training from startup to mastery, featuring practical uses (form letters, newsletters and more), plus advanced topics such as document security and macro creation, sorting and columnar math. Through Version 4.2.

Mastering WordPerfect 5
Susan Baake Kelly
709pp. Ref. 500-X
The revised and expanded version of this definitive guide is now on WordPerfect 5 and covers wordprocessing and basic desktop publishing. As more than 200,000 readers of the original edition can attest, no tutorial approaches it for clarity and depth of treatment. Sorting, line drawing, and laser printing included.

Mastering WordPerfect 5.1
Alan Simpson
1050pp. Ref. 670-7
The ultimate guide for the WordPerfect user. Alan Simpson, the "master communicator," puts you in charge of the latest features of 5.1: new dropdown menus and mouse capabilities, along with the desktop publishing, macro programming, and file conversion functions that have made WordPerfect the most popular word processing program on the market.

Mastering WordPerfect for Windows
Alan Simpson
1100pp. Ref. 806-8
The complete guide to learning, using, and making the most of WordPerfect for Windows. Working with a mouse and the Windows graphical user interface, readers explore every software feature, build practical examples, and learn dozens of special techniques—for macros, data management, desktop publishing, and more.

Mastering WordStar Release 5.5
Greg Harvey
David J. Clark
450pp. Ref. 491-7
This book is the ultimate reference book for the newest version of WordStar. Readers may use Mastering to look up any word processing function, including the new Version 5 and 5.5 features and enhancements, and find detailed instructions for fundamental to advanced operations.

Microsoft Word Instant Reference for the IBM PC
Matthew Holtz
266pp. Ref. 692-8
Turn here for fast, easy access to concise information on every command and feature of Microsoft Word version 5.0—for editing, formatting, merging, style sheets, macros, and more. With exact keystroke sequences, discussion of command options, and commonly-performed tasks.

Practical WordStar Uses
Julie Anne Arca
303pp. Ref. 107-1
A hands-on guide to WordStar and MailMerge applications, with solutions to common problems and "recipes" for day-to-day tasks. Formatting, merge-printing and much more; plus a quick-reference command chart and notes on CP/M and PC-DOS. For Version 3.3.

Teach Yourself WordPerfect 5.1
Jeff Woodward
444pp. Ref. 684-7
Key-by-key instructions, matched with screen-by-screen illustrations, make it possible to get right to work with WordPerfect 5.1. Learn WordPerfect as quickly as you like, from basic editing to merge-printing, desktop publishing, using graphics, and macros.

WordPerfect 5.1 On-Line Advisor Version 1.1
SYBAR, Software Division of SYBEX, Inc.
Ref. 934-X
Now there's no more need to thumb through lengthy manuals. The On-Line Advisor brings you answers to your WordPerfect questions on-screen, right where you need them. For easy reference, this comprehensive on-line help system divides up each topic by key sequence, syntax, usage and examples. Covers versions 5.0 and 5.1. Software package comes with 3½" and 5¼" disks. **System Requirements:** IBM compatible with DOS 2.0 or higher, runs with Windows 3.0, uses 90K of RAM.

Understanding Professional Write
Gerry Litton
400pp. Ref. 656-1

A complete guide to Professional Write that takes you from creating your first simple document, into a detailed description of all major aspects of the software. Special features place an emphasis on the use of different typestyles to create attractive documents as well as potential problems and suggestions on how to get around them.

Understanding WordStar 2000
David Kolodney
Thomas Blackadar
275pp. Ref. 554-9

This engaging, fast-paced series of tutorials covers everything from moving the cursor to print enhancements, format files, key glossaries, windows and MailMerge. With practical examples, and notes for former WordStar users.

Up & Running with Grammatik 2.0
David J. Clark
133pp. Ref. 818-1

Learn to use this sleek new grammar- and style-checking program in just 20 steps. In short order, you'll be navigating the user interface, able to check and edit your documents, customizing the program to suit your preferences, and rating the readability of your work.

Up & Running with PC-Write
Bob Campbell
148pp. Ref. 722-3

This inexpensive capsule introduction to PC-Write covers all the essentials in 20 time-coded "steps"—self-contained lessons that take 15 minutes to an hour to complete. Topics include installation, the menus and help system, basic and advanced editing and formatting techniques, printing, merging, file conversions, and more.

Up & Running with WordPerfect Office/Library PC
Jeff Woodward
142pp. Ref. 717-7

A concise tutorial and software overview in 20 "steps" (lessons of 15 to 60 minutes each). Perfect for evaluating the software, or getting a basic grasp of its features. Learn to use the Office PC shell; use the calculator, calendar, file manager, and notebooks; create macros; and more.

Up & Running with WordPerfect 5.1
Rita Belserene
164pp. Ref. 828-9

Get a fast-paced overview of telecommunications with PROCOMM PLUS, in just 20 steps. Each step takes only 15 minutes to an hour to complete, covering the essentials of creating, editing, saving and printing documents; formatting text; creating multiple-page documents; working with fonts; importing graphic images, and more.

Up & Running with Word for Windows
Bob Campbell
148pp. Ref. 829-7

This fast-paced introduction will have readers using Word for Windows in no time. The book's 20 lessons or "steps" first cover installation and program navigation, then move on to the essentials of text entry, editing, formatting, and printing. Styles, templates, glossaries, macros, outlines, pictures, and merge letters are also covered.

Up & Running with WordPerfect for Windows
Rita Belserene
140pp. Ref. 827-0
Get a fast-paced overview of telecommunications with PROCOMM PLUS, in just 20 steps. Each step takes only 15 minutes to an hour to complete, covering the essentials of creating, editing, saving and printing documents; formatting text; creating multiple-page documents; working with fonts; importing graphic images; more.

WordPerfect 5 Desktop Companion
SYBEX Ready Reference Series
Greg Harvey
Kay Yarborough Nelson
1006pp. Ref. 522-0
Desktop publishing features have been added to this compact encyclopedia. This title offers more detailed, cross-referenced entries on every software feature including page formatting and layout, laser printing and word processing macros. New users of WordPerfect, and those new to Version 5 and desktop publishing will find this easy to use for on-the-job help.

WordPerfect 5 Instant Reference
SYBEX Prompter Series
Greg Harvey
Kay Yarborough Nelson
316pp. Ref. 535-2
This pocket-sized reference has all the program commands for the powerful WordPerfect 5 organized alphabetically for quick access. Each command entry has the exact key sequence, any reveal codes, a list of available options, and option-by-option discussions.

The WordPerfect 5.1 Cookbook
Alan Simpson
457pp. Ref. 680-4
A timesaving goldmine for word processing professionals, this cookbook offers a comprehensive library of sample documents, with exact keystrokes for creating them, and ready-to-use templates on an accompanying disk. Makes full use of version 5.1 features, including PostScript and Laser Jet III support, and covers everything from simple memos to multi-column layouts with graphics.

WordPerfect 5.1 Instant Reference
Greg Harvey
Kay Yarborough Nelson
252pp. Ref. 674-X
Instant access to all features and commands of WordPerfect 5.0 and 5.1, highlighting the newest software features. Complete, alphabetical entries provide exact key sequences, codes and options, and step-by-step instructions for many important tasks.

WordPerfect 5.1 Macro Handbook
Kay Yarborough Nelson
532pp, Ref. 687-1
Help yourself to over 150 ready-made macros for WordPerfect versions 5.0 and 5.1. This complete tutorial guide to creating and using work-saving macros is a must for every serious WordPerfect user. Hands-on lessons show you exactly how to record and use your first simple macros—then build to sophisticated skills.

WordPerfect 5.1 Tips and Tricks (Fourth Edition)
Alan R. Neibauer
675pp. Ref. 681-2
This new edition is a real timesaver. For on-

the-job guidance and creative new uses, this title covers all versions of WordPerfect up to and including 5.1—streamlining documents, automating with macros, new print enhancements, and more.

SPREADSHEETS AND INTEGRATED SOFTWARE

1-2-3 for Scientists and Engineers
William J. Orvis
371pp. Ref. 733-9

This up-to-date edition offers fast, elegant solutions to common problems in science and engineering. Complete, carefully explained techniques for plotting, curve fitting, statistics, derivatives, integrals and differentials, solving systems of equations, and more; plus useful Lotus add-ins.

The ABC's of 1-2-3 (Second Edition)
Chris Gilbert
Laurie Williams
245pp. Ref. 355-4

Online Today recommends it as "an easy and comfortable way to get started with the program." An essential tutorial for novices, it will remain on your desk as a valuable source of ongoing reference and support. For Release 2.

The ABC's of 1-2-3 Release 2.2
Chris Gilbert
Laurie Williams
340pp. Ref. 623-5

New Lotus 1-2-3 users delight in this book's step-by-step approach to building trouble-free spreadsheets, displaying graphs, and efficiently building data-bases. The authors cover the ins and outs of the latest version including easier calculations, file linking, and better graphic presentation.

The ABC's of 1-2-3 Release 2.3
Chris Gilbert
Laurie Williams
350pp. Ref. 837-8

Computer Currents called it "one of the best tutorials available." This new edition provides easy-to-follow, hands-on lessons tailored specifically for computer and spreadsheet newcomers—or for anyone seeking a quick and easy guide to the basics. Covers everything from switching on the computer to charts, functions, macros, and important new features.

The ABC's of 1-2-3 Release 3
Judd Robbins
290pp. Ref. 519-0

The ideal book for beginners who are new to Lotus or new to Release 3. This step-by-step approach to the 1-2-3 spreadsheet software gets the reader up and running with spreadsheet, database, graphics, and macro functions.

The ABC's of Excel on the IBM PC
Douglas Hergert
326pp. Ref. 567-0

This book is a brisk and friendly introduction to the most important features of Microsoft Excel for PC's. This beginner's book discusses worksheets, charts, database operations, and macros, all with hands-on examples. Written for all versions through Version 2.

The ABC's of Quattro Pro 3
Alan Simpson
Douglas Wolf
338pp. Ref. 836-6

This popular beginner's tutorial on Quattro Pro 2 shows first-time computer and spreadsheet users the essentials of electronic number-crunching. Topics range from business spreadsheet design to error-free formulas, presentation slide shows, the database, macros, more.

The Complete Lotus 1-2-3 Release 2.2 Handbook
Greg Harvey
750pp. Ref. 625-1

This comprehensive handbook discusses every 1-2-3 operation with clear instructions and practical tips. This volume especially emphasizes the new improved graphics, high-speed recalculation techniques, and spreadsheet linking available with Release 2.2.

The Complete Lotus 1-2-3 Release 3 Handbook
Greg Harvey
700pp. Ref. 600-6

Everything you ever wanted to know about 1-2-3 is in this definitive handbook. As a Release 3 guide, it features the design and use of 3D worksheets, and improved graphics, along with using Lotus under DOS or OS/2. Problems, exercises, and helpful insights are included.

Lotus 1-2-3 2.2 On-Line Advisor Version 1.1
SYBAR, Software Division of SYBEX, Inc.
Ref. 935-8

Need Help fast? With a touch of a key, the Advisor pops up right on top of your Lotus 1-2-3 program to answer your spreadsheet questions. With over 4000 index citations and 1600 pre-linked cross-references, help has never been so easy to find. Just start typing your topic and the Lotus 1-2-3 Advisor does all the look-up for you. Covers versions 2.01 and 2.2. Software package comes with 3½" and 5¼" disks. **System Requirements:** IBM compatible with DOS 2.0 or higher, runs with Windows 3.0, uses 90K of RAM.

Lotus 1-2-3 Desktop Companion SYBEX Ready Reference Series
Greg Harvey
976pp. Ref. 501-8

A full-time consultant, right on your desk. Hundreds of self-contained entries cover every 1-2-3 feature, organized by topic, indexed and cross-referenced, and supplemented by tips, macros and working examples. For Release 2.

Lotus 1-2-3 Instant Reference Release 2.2 SYBEX Prompter Series
Greg Harvey
Kay Yarborough Nelson
254pp. Ref. 635-9

The reader gets quick and easy access to any operation in 1-2-3 Version 2.2 in this handy pocket-sized encyclopedia. Organized by menu function, each command and function has a summary description, the exact key sequence, and a discussion of the options.

Lotus 1-2-3 Tips and Tricks (2nd edition)
Gene Weisskopf
425pp. Ref. 668-5

This outstanding collection of tips, shortcuts and cautions for longtime Lotus users is in an expanded new edition covering Release 2.2. Topics include macros, range names, spreadsheet design, hardware and operating system tips, data analysis, printing, data interchange, applications development, and more.

COMPANION DISK INFORMATION

PopRef is a convenient DOS utility for laptop computer users. It provides an on-screen list of function keys and commands for common application programs.

At the touch of a user-programmable hot key, PopRef checks what application is running and pops up an appropriate reference screen. When the hot key is released, the reference screen vanishes and the previous screen is instantly restored.

Installation PopRef must be installed on your hard disk using the 3½" disk packaged opposite this page. Just run the INSTALL program from that disk (type **A:INSTALL** to install it from drive A, or **B:INSTALL** to install it from drive B) and follow the on-screen prompts.

Loading Each time you reboot your computer, you should run the PopRef program once to load the utility into memory (type **\SYBEX\POPREF**). If you add this line to your AUTO-EXEC.BAT file, PopRef will be ready automatically whenever you boot.

The Hot Key Combination The default hot-key combination is Alt-spacebar (press and hold down the Alt key, and then press the spacebar). To assign another key to press with Alt, start PopRef with the command **−HOTKEY-*n*,** where *n* is the new key. For example, to set the hot key to Alt-X, type **\SYBEX\POPREF −HOTKEY:X.** The key to press with Alt can be any single letter or digit, as well as the character], [, /, \, or +.

Display To pop up a reference screen, hold down the hot-key combination. It will stay up as long as you hold down the hot key. For a longer look, press Enter while holding down the hot key, and the PopRef screen will remain until you press Esc (the Escape key).

Removal If for any reason you need to remove PopRef from memory, type **\SYBEX\POPREF −R.**